Eco-friendly Home Decor Made Easy

Hacks & Crafts, Fun Zero-Waste DIY Projects for Stylish Homes

HARPER EVERHART

Disclaimer Notice:

Please be aware that the content in this publication is solely for informational and amusement purposes. Every attempt has been made to provide accurate, up-to-date, trustworthy, and comprehensive information. No express or implied guarantees of any sort are made. The reader agrees that the author is not giving expert advice in the areas of law, finance, medicine, or health. This book's content was culled from a number of sources. Before using any of the methods outlined in this book, please seek the advice of a qualified specialist.

By reading this book, the reader acknowledges that the author, including any errors, omissions, or inaccuracies, shall not be held responsible for any direct or indirect loss resulting from the use of the information included herein.

Table of Contents

My Journey to Zero-Waste Lifestyle

It felt like turning the page to a new chapter in my life: *embarking on a zero-waste journey*. It wasn't an epiphany. It was just a tranquil morning that pushed me towards change. It is cluttering all around: broken gadgets, worn-out shoes, and odds and ends that I keep “just in case.” I realized that it was finally time to shift, not just for a tidier space but for a healthier planet. I started with a simple swap of taking plastic bags out and replacing them with reusable ones. It was small, but it felt great. Leaving the shop with colorful cloth bags filled with groceries, one could at least feel that they lived their own way, and it felt so great that I wanted more.

As I kept venturing further into the zero-waste world, the landscape of my entire life began to change. 'Trash' just started to look different. An old jar became my trusty container for leftovers. An old bunch of fabric scraps turned into funky, patchwork covers for my throw pillows. It was so much more than just diverting things from the landfill—it was a quest for creativity and self-discovery. Of course, it wasn't all roses. Disposable culture is hard to fight off, and easy convenience had its grip, sometimes drawing me in for a slip-up. But with every stumble, I got more insight into myself and my habits. It was a trip of trial and error, small choices that added up to significant change.

The transformation in my home was one miracle. I decluttered in a manner that I had never done before; it felt liberating. All of a sudden, empty spaces were my avenues of creativity, and I found myself exercising this philosophy of 'less is more'. I tried a couple of the DIY works, transforming an old glass bottle into a very chic lamp and reclaimed wood into some pretty swanky shelves. Not every single piece stretched the room, but they filled it with character.

Just sharing this journey with other people was absolutely delightful. Friends came to me for tips, and family members were intrigued by my projects. Before I knew it, I was hosting DIY nights, swapping decor ideas, and even organizing local swap meets. My small changes started to spark others' creativity, and we were forming a community.

The journey has not only zero-wasted my home but also myself. Zero-waste is not all about waste; it is just being mindful, learning to appreciate what we have in abundance, and unlocking creativity in quite unexpected ways. It's been a journey of ongoing adventure, packed to the brim with learning and oozing with joy.

And now, it is an open invitation on these pages for you. We're taking the things many consider 'leftovers' and making something meaningful and beautiful for our homes. Together, we can make a difference, one upcycled piece at a time. So come and join me on this exciting journey!

INTRODUCTION

ZERO-WASTE LIFESTYLE

Welcome to your journey toward a zero-waste lifestyle—an adventure that will be personally rewarding for you but also contribute to preserving our beloved planet. Right now, let's see what makes zero-waste important for our homes and the whole world. This is where we will get into the real challenges head-on: how to execute, especially with the pesky ones of squeezing zero-waste habits into tight city apartments and busy urban lifestyles. But fear not—you're not on your own! This book is your loyal friend who will take you through those challenges. We'll show how slight changes can turn around your living spaces and mindset, making your journey to sustainability easy and enjoyable.

Have you ever thought about living a life with zero-waste? It's no fad; it's all about making changes in your life that matter for you and for our beautiful planet. This one act is going to change the way we approach our consumption every day. It helps us pause for a minute, wonder, and ask ourselves, ***"Do I really need this?"*** or ***"Is there a greener option?"*** Such mindfulness can make one easily declutter not only physical space but also the mind, resulting in tranquil, inviting havens. And there's a little bonus: this way of living can be gentle on your pocket as well. We will avoid making superfluous purchases and, because of that, save on the whole of the cost of living. Moreover, the real satisfaction is in living according to the values of ecology and simplicity.

In global terms, the stakes are high, and the choice to go for zero-waste carries a significant impact. One big positive impact is a reduction in the amount of waste that is accumulating in landfills. Imagine all of us deciding to recycle, reuse, or compost—how much landfill space could we save? Plus, by creating less waste, we also save natural resources that would otherwise be used to make new stuff. Oh, and there's the whole pollution and greenhouse gas reduction thing with a side of zero-waste. Incineration facilities and landfills, for example, produce methane, a powerful greenhouse gas. Therefore, diverting our waste from them can only help to keep the air and water cleaner with better choices for the whole ecosystem.

What has shifted is not just the way such lifestyle contributes to the earth in the big picture, but also it pushes businesses to think about the production and packaging of goods differently. Our consumer demand for a sustainable substitute can push companies to practices with less waste and design their production in a way that is durable, not disposable.

Of course, this journey to being zero-waste is not without its struggles—accessibility, cost, and convenience really being the struggles. However, it also becomes another way to unite as one community through the sharing of resources, ideas, and encouragement. It is really powerful to be in unison with other people who are out to make a change for the better. Last but not least, being zero-waste inspires others. Seeing the changes we have made, even a few friends or family members may begin to reevaluate their routines. Because of that, it is shown that sustainable living is possible, and it is very rich in return.

So, I welcome you to a zero-waste lifestyle—let us start this journey together!

Alex – A Young Boy – My Mentor

I met a very brilliant young man named Alex many years ago. He was an app developer, a high-rise flat slap-bang in the middle of the hustle and bustle of the city. Alex would stop every morning for a takeaway coffee in a throwaway cup before going down to the subway. It was an inconspicuous detail, but it struck a heavy blow on the city's waste problem.

On a fateful morning, as he was disposing of his coffee cup, Alex laid his eye on a poster by the subway detailing the grave environmental implications of single-use cups. The information hit him like a ton of bricks when it told him the reality of these cups, often coated with plastic, barely rescued to the recycling bin and found their place in the landfills. This realization finally prompted Alex to make a simple but powerful change: he replaced his disposable cup with a reusable coffee mug. This tiny shift did not only dramatically reduce his daily waste; it actually fired him up for other zero-waste practices. He started using reusable grocery bags at the store, bought refillable water bottles, and even joined a local community-supported agriculture (CSA) group to reduce packaging waste from supermarket produce.

However, Alex's change was more than just inculcated habits. He went further to visit local farmers' markets, where he not only got fresh food but also got into the community, which shared his emerging interest in sustainability. Zero-waste workshops soon became part of his weekly program to learn how to make household cleaners and personal care items, further reducing disposables in his life.

Throughout it all, Alex described to me his ingenious home decorating ideas. It is hard to believe that such a young person can already be so impressive in the art of decoration by repurposing some things to make his apartment look nice. It was a good lesson—never too early or too late in life to learn something new and eco-friendly. Alex learned it from a very young age, and I just stumbled upon it. Yet every one of us took great, if not inordinate, benefits from the trip, proving that it's never too late—or too early—to go on a self-improvement journey that not only enhances your life but also benefits the environment and people around you.

This impression was so influential that it urged me into action. Encouraged by Alex's dedication and real, tangible changes in his lifestyle, I picked up the baton and began promoting, among my friends and colleagues, the zero-waste way of life. His enthusiasm and these visual changes were just so contagious that they became a lighthouse, and the people around him started to look at their habits in a different way. Spotting the potential for even more action on a much broader scale, Alex initiated a workplace challenge on zero-waste and gathered a community of like-minded spirits from our colleagues, who were also willing to make a difference for the planet.

Meet the Challenge

But isn't it a bit weird? You live in the very heart of the city now and think of the zero-waste lifestyle. Are you living in an urban jungle? Maybe that's what growing a garden in a shoebox feels like! But here's the deal: going zero-waste in the city is not only possible but also an exciting adventure. Let's speak about how to turn those problems into your secret weapon!

Let's move on to first up, space or the lack of it, the most ancient urban mystery. How do you make the space for composting or storing bulk items when your apartment is a matchbox? This is where things get crafty. Imagine being able to use your walls for not only photo hanging but also suspending plants or showcasing your labeled jars of bulk goodies. It's as if you're transforming your pad into a functional art exhibit. Besides saving space, vertical gardens bring a touch of nature to your spot, making it cozier.

Now, speaking of the turbocharged pace of this city, convenience is king, right? It seems just a smidgen less taxing to grab a coffee in that throwaway cup than to remember to bring your own. But then again, what if sustainability is the easier, more convenient option? Just pack a zero-waste kit and tuck it into your regular bag: a reusable cup, some cutlery, and maybe a couple of cloth napkins. Treat that kit like something very important, such as car keys or a personal phone. Very shortly, it will be as natural as one of those things: part of your urban survival kit!

And then, there's speed. Life in the city goes by fast, and there's no time to go through recycling or to travel to specialty stores. This is where a dash of tech can really be added. Apps will help show you all the spots for recycling, havens for buying in bulk, and even that quirky thrift shop just around the corner. Plus, sharing the tasks with the neighbors makes the load not only lighter but binds the community even tighter. Speaking of community, cities are hubs for making connections. There's always something going on, which is a great boost for aspiring zero-wasters. Join a community garden, take on a workshop, or launch a swap meet. Urban zones are the boiling cauldrons of ideas and creativity, just as oysters are when giving succor and inspiration.

Yes, city-dwelling zero-waste is a scary proposition initially, but, in truth, it provides a springboard to exciting opportunities. It's all about embracing those constraints and turning them into assets. Each small tweak you make not only jazzes up your digs but also charts a course for a cleaner, greener urban existence. Let's enjoy the ride, be creative in our solutions, and continue to drive towards those small but impactful decisions. Ready to rock your city digs sustainably? Let's do it! Now, let's keep that in mind as we dig deep into this conversation—grappling with these challenges, not to brace for tough times, but to gear up and convert every hurdle into a springboard towards a more sustainable lifestyle. Even the coziest of spaces can bloom into a showcase of zero-waste living with a touch of creativity, a dollop of persistence, and a sprinkle of community backing.

How This Book Helps

All Set to Go Zero-Waste in Your Urban Hustle, Are You? Surely, as a good reader, you are already considering how to begin this eco-friendly process in your cozy apartment. Worry not! Picture this book as your smart neighbor and a bunch of wisdom about living in the city, just at your hand, always there to give you a push or answer your question. Consider this book your city-dwelling zero-waste toolkit, chock-full of advice that's totally doable for urbanites like you. We'll run through everything—from finding ways to cram a recycling bin into your already-tiny kitchen to locating creative ways to compost without a backyard. And no, we won't cramp your style or gobble up your precious space.

Time to get on with some projects.

I filled this book with just rad do-it-yourself projects for small spaces. Nothing like those kinds of crafts; they are fun, hip, and completely doable, even if you don't consider yourself much of a crafter. Imagine turning that stack of magazines into a cool lampshade or the ugly old dresser into a vintage masterpiece. Imagine no more; I'll walk you through the whole thing, step by step, so you can personalize your space without filling up the garbage. Now, moving closer to zero waste sometimes can feel a bit lonely, especially when it seems like everybody else is cruising along business as usual. That's why I've woven in stories from some real folk who've been exactly where you are. They've cracked the code to make zero-waste clicks in the hustle and bustle of city living. These stories are here to uplift, motivate, and perhaps even give you a chuckle now and then. It's like having a gang of friends there, cheering you on as you go through this journey. And hey, count me in too!

When you hit a block, just crack open this book; a zero-waste cleaner, crafty storage of bulk goods, this is your go-to guide. This book is your trusty sidekick, ever present to navigate you through those everyday choices that, believe it or not, wield a huge environmental impact. By the time you hit the last page, you're no longer just another urban dweller. No, sir, you are a zero-waste crusader, making all the right, sustainable choices that are revolutionizing not only your abode but your entire city-living experience. You look at your neighborhood in a different way—every turn is another opportunity for sustainability. Ready to don the eco-cape and live the zero-waste lifestyle? Let's dive into the first chapter of our new lifestyle.

CHAPTER 1

THE ZERO-WASTE MINDSET

Welcome aboard the first chapter of your journey into sustainability. This chapter will help to set the base for you, equipping you with a sort of mindset and tools that are imperative to your journey toward a greener lifestyle. Brace yourself to realize how a mere shift in perspective could wield a profound impact on our planet.

First off is the Art of Reframing: turning society's notion of garbage into something valuable. All of this can change everything, whereby you'll be able to unlock hidden potentials of what others find to be waste, hence revolutionizing your interaction with materials that flow throughout your life.

Then, we will move on to the Power of Incremental Changes, which will clarify how significant every small change is within the context of waste reduction. You will realize that even a small decision by one person may have a big impact on the fight against the waste of our Earth. This section will be empowering in the sense that it will make you aware of how the smallest things can feed a bigger solution.

Lastly, we build Your Zero-Waste Arsenal—the key tools and knowledge base you need to set up before you begin your zero-waste journey. Starting from where to get the right kind of materials, this toolkit will help you figure out just how you can bring tangible changes to your daily routine.

Piecing them together develops a no-waste attitude, transforming the theory into practical habits that are good for your home and our Earth. So, let's start this really exciting journey of changing our waste approach and revealing the changes that we can make with our own hands.

Shifting Your Perspective

This is the single most meaningful, pivotal step along the way to living zero-waste. It's real waste reduction, understanding the potential that things have that would be normally thrown away as disposable — a perspective that is really changing my life toward a more sustainable approach.

On adopting the philosophy of zero-waste, my apartment was full of refuse that I had kept—old magazines, jars, old clothes, and even defunct electronics. Originating in waste, those items changed the moment I realized the philosophy of zero-waste. Instead of realizing them as refuse, I started looking at them as reservoirs of untapped potential. Consider something as simple as glass jars, which I have been tossing into the recycling bin for years; I suddenly saw them in a new light as multi-purpose vessels. They had become my planters, storage for all those bulk pantry items, or beautiful lanterns casting soft ambient light. This new way of looking at things restored my power to reduce waste and improve my space with zero expense.

In that same vein, even the old magazines and newspapers that were read once and thrown into the recycling box seemed to have new lives. Whether turned into one-of-a-kind handcrafted paper beads or used for custom-wrapped gifts, the colorful pages would take on new life, personalized to be treasured by the receiver. Each page turned into a canvas of what could be created for beauty and function.

The clothes themselves, unfit to be donated, would be turned into fabric yarn for crochet projects or cut into strips for rag rugs. It, in turn, sparked a new hobby and turned my home into a repository for handmade, green-conscious decorations heavy with a sense of individuality. This kind of Zero-waste Mindset has given me a true appreciation for the constant abundance all around. What was genuinely inspiring was the creativity and innovation that it could stimulate, all while reminding me of the very real effect my actions have on the environment. Instead of lots of landfills with my contributions, I found new and exciting ways to reuse existing resources. This paradigm shift took a slow course of evolution. One jar at a time, one magazine at a time, one clothing piece at a time. However, with the acceptance of these baby steps, my vision experienced an earthquake; no longer could I see store shelves as just a collection of products but as stockpiles of unprocessed materials awaiting my next project.

As I walked along, it was trash day in my neighborhood, and trash stuff had stopped being garbage and turned into treasures waiting to be upcycled. Among the most transformative changes was in my kitchen, which had been inefficiently cluttered by most standards, largely due to the small size of the urban surroundings. Zero-waste life has inspired my mind to reinvent this culinary space. For me, blank walls were just a canvas on which to hang vertical herb gardens. Repurposed bottles became dispensers for water, and mismatched containers began to do double duty as charmingly eclectic storage solutions. This not only optimized the space but went further, transitioning my kitchen into a showroom of eco-conscious living. It goes beyond practicality; it even gives meaning and narrative from the objects, which are related so closely to the environment. Craftsmanship means making something with your hands out of what was doomed to oblivion materials and bringing the connection with one's environment that is based on respect and ingenuity.

These ways of thinking did provoke feelings of community. Local swap meets, crafting collectives, and even upcycling forums did bring me to those with whom I could feel the same way when seeing the world full of potential. We talked ideas out, we celebrated victories together, and we supported missions between us to live a more sustainable life. It made this community feel invaluable—an inspiration, a driving force, and a home all the way. Knowing that other travelers were having similar visions made the expedition much less daunting and much more doable. It was a collective odyssey, meaning that the challenging task of not producing waste was shared.

So, when you start with your own perspective shift, do remember that every small step is a cog in the larger machine of sustainability. Let's start with a small exercise. Start by looking critically at your home setting. Think of jars, papers, and old clothes not as trash but as parts of a zero-waste haven. Start experimenting with ways of doing things using what you have, share successes and failures, and be a part of a community that grows creativity and resourcefulness. You will not only be renovating your space but also literally changing your world by altering your way of looking at the things around you. This is zero-waste in the mind's eye: to see not what things are but what they could be. What it actually underscores is that most of the time, the solution to our waste problem doesn't lie in making new things but in reimagining what already exists.

Small Steps, Big Impact

Taking baby steps in the greener way of living doesn't connote making minute changes; it means knowing its profound impact on both one's life and the well-being of the planet. This should lightly nudge a change of attitude, creating hope for a more sustainable and brighter future. My journey towards zero-waste began with such a small and inconspicuous step that it amounted to nothing except the obvious fact that one day, I decided to quit plastic water bottles. It did seem to me like just a small step, but in fact, it was the decisive one toward a bigger green end. Every refill in my own bottle was a representative of less plastic counterpart headed to the landfills—a small change to kickstart my eco-conscious journey.

That first change led to more small decisions. I began to take reusable bags into the store and to choose products with less packaging. I even started to make my own household cleaners. Each step seemed quite small on its own, but when I added them all together, I could see I was making a real difference. It was amazing how these tiny little habits if stacked, began to change not only my daily routines but also my perspective on the world. For the first time, I began to see the real power of these small measures when I saw them have a ripple effect on others. When I threw a no-waste dinner party complete with real plates and silverware, others started thinking about taking such waste-saving actions in their own lives. It was indicative of how contagious small steps can be and of how transformable collective action is.

It is through this journey that I have learned how small choices can have such immense consequences. Each 'refuse,' 'reduce,' 'reuse,' or 'recycle' has contributed a lot to the knowledge that I have acquired on the deep influence that we can have through conscious consumption. What is more, it has proved indispensable to share these triumphs and tribulations. The record of my zero-waste adventures has created a camaraderie with others working toward a similar end. This community was my cheering squad, my sounding board, my well of inspiration. It is proof of the power of story, of just how motivating and upholding a force can be, not just for oneself but for each other.

Therefore, when you are beginning your adventure of waste reduction, just keep in mind that everything starts with a small and sometimes even insignificant change. It may seem minor in the big scheme, but it sets off a domino effect of transformation. By changing small parts of what are normal routines for us, we not only have less of an ecological footprint but rather inspire a collective movement. That is the beauty of starting small; it affirms that capacity within us to, at some point, one tiny choice at a time, finally make meaningful change. Let's continue making those incremental decisions since they have the power to spark huge shifts in our communities and beyond.

Building Your Zero-Waste Toolkit

Now that you are off to a great start by rebuilding your mindset and seeking the unseen values in things once thrown away as garbage, it is time to check what is deep down there inside you, the next important core part of your zero-waste adventure: building your arsenal. It is not the type of arsenal one generally relates to as a physical tool, but, in the context of this guide, it relates to the set of knowledge and resources that will come in critical when it comes to the realization of your zero-waste ideas, most importantly, in the creation of beautiful, purpose-driven products for your home. Quickly, at the onset of my zero-waste making, I realized the critical importance of having on hand the right tools and materials. What's more, it has been one of the best examples of efficiency and effectiveness in thinking up new ways to use what you already have. So, let's take a deeper look into building your own zero-waste toolkit, which includes items to have and resources on how to get your hands on them.

Understanding the Essentials

What you include in your zero-waste kit will depend in part on what specifically within the project you're interested in, but there are a few basic items that can be useful no matter what.

- ***Fine Cutting Tools***: Among the first items to invest in are a good pair of scissors. Whether the scissors will be used for cutting old clothes, cleaning rags, cutting old clothes up for fabric to patch with, or cutting paper for labeling, the scissors will make those tasks easier and more precise. In addition, a utility knife or hobby blade will be useful for cutting through tougher materials such as cardboard or thick plastics.
- ***Durable Storage Containers***: I suggest using a mixture of recycled jars and crates, with some old furnishings repurposed for keeping a variety of items from fasteners and hardware to ribbons and fabric remnants. This will also be good, as the clear containers are very convenient, as one can just look at them without opening them to see what is inside.
- ***Basic Sewing Kit***: If someone isn't very talented with a needle and thread, the tools are still good to have, including needles, thread, pins, and an assortment of buttons. They turn out to be useful in a surprising number of applications, not only in making things of fabric but also in quick repairs that may extend the life of a surprising number of articles.
- ***An Assortment of Adhesives***: A variety of adhesives are absolutely necessary. A good hot glue gun makes fast, sturdy

bonds between many materials; green craft glue and double-sided tape are critical for myriad uses.

- ***Paints and Brushes***: Aesthetic enhancement is frequently part and parcel of upcycling efforts, and new paint can be quite transformative. Water-based paints are easy to wash and have less chemical content. A variety of brushes will suit different finishes and detailing requirements right from complicated to minute.

Finding Your Materials

Now, what are you supposed to do in order to find all of these necessary tools and materials? Well, the first thing I did was to look around my own house and discover things hidden deep inside the drawers or at the very bottom of closets. You would not believe how much stuff just waits to be repurposed in your very own home. Then, I spent most of my time in thrift stores and garage sales, finding potential tools and materials that one could take and make into something new.

Online markets are another great resource. They are inexpensive since people more often get rid of or sell at the lowest price the same products you are looking for. Always check on such platforms before buying something new—it saves you money and cuts down on the waste produced. The brands selected under tools and materials for your zero-waste toolkit make a huge difference in the quality of the items you are making as well as in the durability of those items. Personal Experience with Building My Toolkit

Building my toolkit has been one long trial-and-error adventure. I remember purchasing a set of old, rusted tools from a garage sale. They appeared dilapidated. However, cleaning and sharpening them made them just suitable for my needs. That was a small win, but it taught me to see the potential where others see nothing but neglect.

As you gather your collection of tools and materials, be sure to consider the space in your dwelling. Starting with no real crafting space, my first priority was for tools that could be kept in a small space. A collapsible worktable and stackable containers helped me to maximize space while keeping up with my crafting capabilities. Now, armed with your toolkit, you are ready to create. Every tool and material in your kit holds the power to transform garbage into something beautiful. With each use, not only will you beautify your living space, but you will also make a firm commitment to be a zero-waste denizen.

Just remember, the purpose here is not just to give you tools but to inspire your imagination so you can begin to see the potential where, before, there was nothing but discard. Each piece saved from the edge of the trash and transformed into some sort of home ornament or usable furnishing is one more piece helping to create a sustainable environment. In addition to your ability to create things, you get to do it with heart, a realization of your zero-waste principles.

CHAPTER 2

ASSESSING AND REDUCING YOUR WASTE

Starting on our zero-waste journey will mean taking an up-close look at our living spaces and our everyday actions. We're going to do a Home Waste Audit, one that's similar to running our homes' investigation ourselves. *It's like a spy game!* Information derived from this audit can help us make smart changes to reduce waste. We will then go into Waste Reduction Strategies, which are simple strategies that, no matter how busy one's life is, can be implemented to help make the path toward sustainability a walk in the park. We will also get acquainted with the term Minimalism as, in detail, we learn how this guiding principle can help us with our lives in a really profound and enriching way. Through simplification and focusing on the essence, we clean our minds and our living surroundings, reduce to the minimum, and make our zero-waste commitment even stronger.

Conducting a Home Waste Audit

When we understand transitioning into a more sustainable lifestyle, the next obvious thing is understanding where all this waste is really coming from. A Home Waste Audit changes from being a dreary task to an exciting voyage of discovery and transformation.

Think of this as a scavenger hunt, not for treasure troves, but for things that can be rescued from the trash—and the finds are often no less than treasures. In identifying the major waste sources from our homes, we not only see how and where we consume but also how we can bring this to a drastically low rate of environmental impact.

Discovering Your Waste Patterns

It can be very detective work. Begin by looking at what you throw out each day and each week. The result can sometimes be shocking! For instance, when I first started down the zero-waste path, I was amazed at the amount of food packaging items that were residing in my trash can. Cereal boxes, plastic bags, and even bags that contain frozen vegetables. Another big culprit? *Disposable cleaning supplies*, like sponges and paper towels, which I used profusely—without even a second thought. You can easily do this by categorizing waste over a week or so into some segments, let's say, plastics, organics, paper, glass, and miscellaneous. You can use separate bins or just have labeled bags. It's easy to see what types of waste you most often end up with because of the visual separation.

One Week Waste Audit

I finished my first week-long audit, and the findings started back unabashed. Plastics everywhere. It wasn't just in food packaging, but it found its way into anything from a bottle of shampoo to a bag of snacks. That was my call to change. When the physical manifestation of waste was thrown at me, the compulsion for change hit hard. Then, I researched replacements for the most common items in my waste bins. Food packaging: I tried to buy in bulk when possible and bring my own containers to stores with that option. For cleaning products, I have become a huge fan of reusable clothes and have concocted some homemade cleaning solutions without packaging that can only be used once.

Implementing Sustainable Practices

The adoption of these changes wasn't an immediate affair; it demanded a mind switch coupled with a touch of creativity. Initially, finding a substitute for paper towels in this innovation felt daunting. I discovered that I could cut old T-shirts into squares, and that provided the most simple and efficient replacement. It did not only help reduce expenses but also the waste I was generating. These cloths could be washed over and over again and reused, which would dramatically reduce the number of paper towel rolls I buy per year. The next significant area was food waste. I started composting, so now, instead of waste, I created something useful. I was expecting that starting a compost bin would be more of a chore, but it turned out to be very easy, and I even had amazing compost to put into my garden.

Engaging the Community

As I made these changes, I shared them with my friends and neighbors. Many of them followed the same, which created curiosity and even zeal in many. This way of sharing ideas and practices not only spread the zero-waste ideal through the community but also made the process more rewarding and less daunting. I even did workshops and group meetings to acquaint people with the idea of waste audits and how a few small changes would really start to make a difference. These were not just interactions for knowledge acquisition but also the making of a network of support from which we would learn about others' struggles.

Personal Reflections and Continuous Improvement

Reflecting on my initial setbacks, the learning process gradually led me to minimize waste, and therefore, zero-waste living is seen as a continuing process. It is always filled with constant changes and reconsiderations. Each time I bring something into my home, either with a gift or an essential purchase, sometimes new forms of waste come along, and each time, I take it as a challenge to search for new solutions. This cycle of audit and correction has become a fixed part of my daily life. Its rewards go far beyond the initial expectations I had, shaping not only my physical surroundings but revolutionizing my mind toward consumption and waste. Here is your chance to start looking at your garbage from a totally different angle. It is not just disposal but understanding, managing, and eventually preventing it.

This section provides the foundation to bring these understandings to work and convert them into concrete steps toward realizing a zero-waste home—one trash spared at a time. Maybe, by now, you're looking at your garbage bin in a new way, where there was only garbage before. Remember, for each one of these items saved from the landfill, you're working toward helping make this a sustainable world. So, let's keep pushing the limits of what we can do in our homes, using this new information to implement day-to-day changes that really make a difference for the environment.

Waste Reduction Strategies

Now that we know where our trash is coming from, it's time to get down to business and tackle this thing. Reducing waste isn't all about taking giant steps; in fact, sometimes it's the smaller, everyday decisions that have the largest impact. I want to present a few specific ideas for making less trash. With each one, I've included a story from someone who's given it a whirl. While some of the tips will likely appeal to you more than others, don't be disheartened if one seems too difficult to implement in your situation. There is always another way to explore, and every step on the way is a learning opportunity within the stride to a zero-waste lifestyle.

Tip 1: Say Goodbye to Single-Use Plastics

One of the simplest but most effective ways to help reduce waste is to say goodbye to disposable plastics in your daily life. These include things like plastic bags, straws, coffee cups, and water bottles. Use reusables wherever it is possible: shopping bags, metal straws, your favorite coffee mug, and that indestructible water bottle of yours.

Real-life Example: Emily, a friend and fellow graduate, had the chance to learn and appreciate the idea of wiping out single-use plastics from her life after she attended the sustainability workshop with me. She took a pact with me to completely eliminate disposable plastic from our lives. Emily started out by changing the plastic water bottles for a nice, shiny, stainless steel one, and then went on to invest in a set of reusable shopping bags and a collapsible coffee cup that she kept in her backpack at all times. It took some getting used to in order to remember all these things to carry every day; however, she set some reminders in her phone, and it soon became second nature. Soon, Emily not only reduced her own waste but also inspired people around her. She even started a mini-campaign in the apartment building to use more reusables, showing the stylish alternatives she purchased.

Motivation for You: Start by picking one of the single-use plastic items you use a lot and find something reusable to replace it that resonates with you. Put them in a place that you will see right before you leave—or even better, someplace you will use them, such as your car, office, or bag. And don't worry if you miss a few days. Habit change is really about practice, not perfection. Stick to it, and it will be automatic pretty soon. And remember, every small change you make adds up to make a big difference. Believe me, you're gonna feel awesome and great that your efforts are actually doing something.

Tip 2: Opt for Reusable Containers

Another ideal switch for less waste is to cut out disposable containers and wrapping. Say goodbye to sandwich bags or cling film and swap them out for beeswax wraps or airtight containers. They are perfect for leftovers, taking lunch to work, or shopping in the bulk section.

Real-life Example: Meet Mark. He is an old buddy and a fellow food enthusiast. He has recently gone on this mission to reduce waste in his kitchen. It was "a coffee chat about kitchen waste," which inspired Mark to make some new arrangements. So, he purchased glass containers for himself and began using beeswax wraps for his sandwiches and snacks. He did say it was a bit of a faff at first, the inconvenience of extra dishwashing and the lack of cling film. Even the placement of glass jars in the refrigerator and the much superior taste of their contents carried their own argumentative force. Mark shared that more than anything else, those changes made his food last much longer, so his environmentally friendly behaviors became the talk of his office and even influenced discussions on similar behaviors. They started to adopt.

Motivation for You: Start with one type of reusable container that will fit into your lifestyle: a few glass jars or a set of silicone lids, for example. Just keep adding to it when you're finally feeling good about the ways you're using reusables. You really do have to take it slowly to make it sustainable for you. Most importantly, every small stride contributes to the overall image of waste reduction. At first, it may appear to be a bit of a hassle, but continue making it a habit, and you'll find that using reusables is just as convenient as it is for the environment.

Tip 3: Compost Organic Waste

Composting is such a powerful means of waste reduction. Actually, composting food waste, coffee grinds, and even paper towels can divert quite a bit of waste out of landfills, making not just nutritious soil for garden use or house plants.

Real-life Example: Think of Sarah, a city-dweller living in an apartment who thought that composting was not possible in her urban setting at the onset. However, after our lunchtime discussion about how even a city dweller could get into composting, she felt motivated to do it. With an under-counter, space-saving compost bin with automatic odor control, Sarah began working composting into her daily routine. Though the additional segregation of organic waste appeared to be an added task, she found it became part of her routine quite fast. She was satisfied by donating her compost to a community garden to which she belonged, and the organic waste she recycled served to enrich the soil for their vegetable plots. She found a lot of joy in seeing how her food scraps turned into useful soil for the growth of food to be used locally. This was an embodied link of her urban existence to the natural cycle of growth and renewal.

Motivation for You: If composting piques your interest, why not begin with a basic bin in your kitchen? Alternately, look into local composting services if managing a bin seems more than you could take on. Don't stress yourself with being perfect from the start. If you are like Sarah, you will have growing pains first — but you'll see, it pays off. With small, regular steps, you'll start to see impactful positives from composting. Not only does it minimize your waste output, but it is a way of creating wastes that, when put into nature, can re-enrich the environment and bring about immense satisfaction. Dive into it and experience how even the smallest of kitchen scraps save the world from turning much greener.

Tip 4: Buy Second Hand

Another reason for buying second-hand is that it not only saves you money but is also a noble cause to buy waste. Most thrift stores, online markets, or local swap meets may carry clothes, furniture, and even electronics that are in really good condition.

Real-Life Example: Laura, the retired schoolteacher and close friend, changed her shopping habits after coming to a local thrift store with me about five years ago. She was doubtful at first, thinking it was below her standards and a bit too much work, but thrifting quickly became a passion for her, too. She saw it for herself: how she could easily find quality, character-rich pieces for her home without contributing to the fast consumerism cycle. And now her living space is a treasure trove of vintage finds, all tastefully furnished so that each piece tells a unique story, adding charm and significance. Personally, every time I'm back visiting, we'll sit together over our tales of recent discoveries; Laura tells of how rewarding it is to give these pieces a new lease on life.

Motivation for You: The next time you need to shop for some furniture, an outfit, or a gadget, try making it a point to first see if you can get a secondhand item. Visit some thrift stores in your area, go to online classifieds, or take part in communal swap meets. This will undoubtedly involve more time and effort, but the chase can be exciting—and the payoffs valuable. You not only get to find interesting and very affordable things, but you also actively help reduce waste and lessen demand for new items. Embrace the fun of thrift store shopping, and love the stories and savings that come along with every find.

Tip 5: Reduce Paper Usage

Going paperless is not just about going digital; it is being mindful of every piece of paper you come into contact with, whether it's in the kitchen or the office.

Real-life Example: Think of Jenny, a former co-worker way back when I was in the graphic design trenches, who seriously cut back on her paper waste. She learned from an office waste reduction workshop and now had dual-sided printing at home with her printer settings and digital tools for taking notes and sketching. She replaced paper towels at home with cloth napkins and reusable cleaning cloths. Adaptation caused her some difficulties in the very beginning, especially during the meetings that went in no time and required digital notetaking, but Jenny eventually said that it was what made her more productive and organized. She shared with me that she reduced paper waste to nearly nothing, not to mention sparking curiosity and similar steps among her colleagues, leading to noticeable drops in paper consumption in our office.

Motivation for You: Aim for an easy one to start with, for example, cutting paper use in half. Where and what can you substitute disposable paper for reusable options, or better yet, find a digital option? Whether it is printing less, integrating cloth napkins into your regular rotation, or even using apps for lists instead of a pen and a piece of paper, all those tiny changes eventually add up. Keep in mind that transitioning to reduced paper is a work in progress, and patience and determination are needed to develop these new habits. Each of your every step counts not only in promoting health for the planet but also in a way to influence others through your example. So, keep moving further, celebrating every milestone passed.

Remember that putting these strategies into practice is a process that unfolds slowly. It has taken me a while to find what works and to experience changes from it. Those small shifts would make such a big difference in my life and mind around resources. ***The key is in the word: try on, adjust***. The way you will embrace a zero-waste lifestyle is personal and individual, and it makes a difference with every tiny step you take. Just keep trying these tips and celebrating all the little victories. You aren't just throwing trash away, but you are setting an example for a more sustainable and aware way of living.

Embracing Minimalism

After looking at a few effective ways of reducing waste and embracing a sustainable style of living, you may wonder what is next in your zero-waste life journey. The answer to that probably does lie in the philosophy of minimalism, where ***less is indeed more***. But it's not just about decluttering your physical space; it's also about simplifying life and making conscious decisions that tell others about your commitment to living with less waste and in defense of *Mother Nature*.

The Beauty of Minimalism

Embracing minimalism doesn't mean stark, empty living spaces; it doesn't mean depriving oneself of happiness. Minimalism is more about just placing a lot of emphasis on those things that add value to one's life: finding beauty and abundance in simplicity, giving worth to quality more than quantity, and creating space for things that really matter.

A Personal Shift to Minimalism

I remember so vividly the sense of stress that overcame me when looking at the sheer amount of things a couple of years ago during a spring cleaning exercise inspired by my zero-waste living journey. In questioning the very need for these items, I realized most were being held onto out of sentimentality or fear of needing it one day. The fact was, most of the things had not been touched in years and had taken up real estate within my physical and mental space. I went about it slowly, purging one room at a time. I gave away clothes I had not worn in years, responsibly recycled broken electronics, and took to the library books I did not care for anymore. The purge itself was very liberating, and it educated me, making me realize patterns of consumption and, therefore, wiser towards the acquisition of new possessions.

Living with Less

A minimalist approach actually has very real, material consequences for how much we're sending off to the landfill. Each thing you don't get is one less thing that could wind up there. I now have a whole slew of questions I ask myself before making a purchase: Do I actually need this thing? Can I borrow it or find it used? If I need it new, can I find it with minimal or responsibly sourced materials? Ever since I started to ask those questions, my consumption has diminished remarkably, and so has the waste I produce.

Embracing Quality Over Quantity

One of the essential ideas of minimalism is to go for ***quality rather than quantity***. It will be about high-quality goods owned in smaller numbers. Buying fewer quantities of higher quality items increases their lifespan and lessens the number of times they need to be replaced, thus cutting down on waste and, in many instances, it becomes cost-efficient in the long run.

A Real-Life Example

The story of Sarah entering into placing more emphasis on quality rather than quantity includes an experience in buying a high-quality blender.

❖ ***Sarah's Journey into Quality***

Sarah had just started working as a graphic designer and wanted to follow her health routine but was finding it difficult to prepare balanced meals every day. To ensure that, she opted to take smoothies, which could only be prepared using a blender. While at it, she went ahead and purchased cheap blenders under the assumption that they would save her some money. To her disappointment, they broke down after just a few months of use, causing Sarah to lose her smoothie, waste her money, and go through the extra hustle of unplanned purchases again. Such cases normally contribute to the piling up of refuse in landfills.

❖ ***Quality Choice***

After breaking a set of 3 blenders in as many years, Sarah knew something had to change. At one sustainability workshop in a community center, she learned that the way she was buying stuff was making her life more stressful and the cause of environmental degradation. Stories of other people inspired Sarah to research the market where the blenders she would go for would be really durable, work great, and be produced following environmentally friendly practices.

❖ ***Research and Purchase***

Sarah had spent weeks researching the difference between models, reading all the reviews, and tearing apart the companies' promises of sustainability. She wanted a powerful and effective blender with a long-lasting warranty and pledged itself to green production. Finally, she spent more money than ever before and bought a high-end blender with a ten-year warranty.

❖ *Lasting Impact of Her Choice*

It's been 5 years now, and Sarah's blender can still work like it was just bought yesterday. What was bought has paid off because it lasted, plus it gave Sarah peace of mind. Yet, what's more, its unshakable nature has kept Sarah also eating healthily, which contributes much to her well-being in general.

❖ *Influence on Others*

Sarah's decision to choose quality over quantity made her social circle re-evaluate their own consumption behavior. As those around her began to see her success, they latched onto that quality and started to create durability and sustainability within their own purchase habits. Sarah went on to be an advocate for quality investments, sharing her story to inspire others to think long-term about their purchasing decisions. And she was, in essence, taking to heart the crux of minimalism: satisfaction that endures and environmental stewardship over the false virtue of savings now. That change of mindset is part and parcel of going zero-waste, which reduces waste not in terms of refuse but in terms of constant consumption.

The Impact of Fewer Possessions

Fewer belongings will reduce the cleanliness and organization of living space; this could very well be among the main ideas behind zero-waste. Less stuff means less cleaning or maintenance, which means a calmer ambiance that is in tune with sustainable living. This kind of setting correlates with surroundings and values, which will lead to a lifestyle that has less waste.

Motivation to Act: Begin by evaluating things in your home, ideally by category, for example, clothing, kitchen gadgets, or tools. Determine what you really do and do not need, and consider throwing out extra things that belong to you. This decluttering process will free up not only physical space but also mental clutter and, therefore, stress.

Long-Term Benefits of Minimalism

In my case, minimalism helps not only reduce the waste that is created but also maintain heightened sustainability and find a more creative solution in problem-solving than by relying on consumption. A path toward minimalism is progressive: it can change with evolving needs and aspirations for sustainable living. Give this experiment a go at reducing possessions and witness if this really impacts the amount of waste you generate. You will surely find that having less is indeed very satisfactory, and it helps you and the Earth.

Your Turn to Embrace Less

Consider how minimalism can contribute to your life. It doesn't have to be all-out; small steps lead to big leaps. Give it a shot; check the results for yourself, and, of course, remember: it's a process. It will definitely work out for you in reducing waste and improving your quality of life. I believe you will find that by merely reducing your possessions to what truly brings you value, you automatically support a much more sustainable, zero-waste lifestyle.

CHAPTER 3

SOURCING AND COLLECTING MATERIALS

Are you ready to roll up your sleeves, wuddle through the enjoyment of hunting material for your next DIY project, and transform it into delightful home decor? In this chapter, we'll delve into different creative sources from which you can draw hidden treasures waiting to be upcycled. And then we'll figure out how to keep things neat and accessible so you're poised for those ***"hit me like a bolt of lightning"*** crafting ideas. Safety is paramount, and we'll cover the basics of how to handle the stuff. Whether you consider yourself an upcycling expert or you are just new to the game, this chapter has all the basics to ensure your crafting is fun and Earth-healthy. Let the scavenger hunt for crafting treasures begin!

Where to Find Recyclable Materials

Have you paused to look at how much stuff there is for creative reuse available in your house or just in your local area? It's kind of like a superpower—seeing possibilities where others might just see garbage. As you progress on this leg of your zero-waste journey, look at everything as though it were just a piece for your next home decor project. We will look at beginning your adventure in material collection and turning the ordinary into the extraordinary.

Let's start from the closest place: your home. In your house lays a landfill of items waiting to be revived. Take, for instance, those chipped or mismatched ceramic plates; rather than trashing them, why not have them make a mosaic table top? Worn-out curtains or tablecloths could be transformed into colorful cushion covers or a bouncy patchwork throw. And *what about those old CDs or DVDs you've got lying around the house*? You can upcycle them into reflective mosaics, coasters, or wall art. Even those tech world gadgets that are called old school have some amazing parts in them, from the buttons to the screens, that could be great interactive art or funky décor.

If you exhaust all your searching in your own home, further expand your search to your local neighborhood. Small local businesses usually have materials that they have in excess and do not mind giving them away. For example, the local carpenter might have some spare wood that you can use to create small shelving units, or a bike shop down the street could have old tires and chains for you to create furniture or garden art with. Don't be afraid to ask since most of the shop owners are usually interested or excited about zero-waste projects.

The garage sales and flea markets are also the prime places for upcycle items. This is all about seeing a vintage suitcase or an antique lamp and what could be done with them to make unique home decorating pieces. Engaging in community sales does not only boost community camaraderie but also lessens what goes to landfills.

Connecting with Community Resources

Sometimes, what one man regards as trash is another man's treasure, and so on and so forth. You might even be able to find people giving away big items, such as furniture, for free. These might be great for your bigger creative projects!

In a zero-waste crafting world, it's kind of like finding some hidden oasis to get to use some of the community resources that go overlooked. Check for online swapping groups and your local *Buy Nothing* community. These spots are literally goldmines for free stuff. Every day, someone like you or me posts things they have that they would like to give away in the hope that someone else can use them. It's a great way to take things out of landfills and find something interesting and useful to you without spending one cent.

And don't leave aside those local crafting circles and workshops. Think about hanging out with some of your neighbors who are all into doing things by themselves. You can exchange materials with each other, share some tips, and maybe even learn how to do something new together. Some of these events can be found in local community centers or libraries; sometimes, the materials are even provided.

Better yet, speak with the locals in small businesses and craft stores who are in your area. I bet most of them have way too many supplies that they don't know what to do with. For example, one casual talk with a local woodworker might end up in a gold mine of beautiful wood scraps, just perfect for the next project. Or what about the local seamstresses? They might have containers full of fabric scraps just waiting for a new life.

Community gardens and environmental organizations offer a vast, sustainable pool of activity sources. Community gardens also often host workshops on learning skills like composting and crafting garden art out of recyclable objects. It also provides a good opportunity to come closer to like-minded people who have enthusiasm for sustainability.

And don't forget the resources of your local public library or schools. Libraries often have bulletin boards full of information about things that are coming up, and they may even have loan tools and books packed with how-to information. School art departments are another great resource — students and teachers almost surely have supplies or project scraps they are happy to part with.

How do you use all these resources? Simple: you just get into it! Join those online groups, meet your neighbors at the meetups, and never shy away from asking local business owners. The more you get into it, the more you will find your community teeming with opportunities and assets waiting to be tapped. Get your explorer's hat on and start your adventure in community resource discovery. You will score great stuff for your next project and meet a network of other people who are concerned about the environment. You'll be able to help each other out and help the planet—one reused item at a time. And believe me, it is as fulfilling as it is fun!

Attending Specialized Workshops

Have you ever considered attending a workshop that teaches you how to upcycle old items into stunning decor pieces? It's not just a new hobby but more like gaining behind-the-scenes access to the world of creative upcycling. Many community centers, libraries, and local artisans have these types of hands-on workshops. These are not your typical crafty sessions; they are hands-on, practical, and super fun!

Imagine: A Saturday morning in one of those local studios where you learn how to make fancy lamps from old thrown-away glass bottles or how to make nice wallets from old book covers. Best of all, you would carry those beautifully made products home with you. Now, you were not only a recipient of new décor but also of skills and knowledge to continue making them on your own.

Here is a little secret: these workshops are great for networking with other creative minds. The exchange of tips, tricks, and ideas from like-minded souls can be most inspiring, much like refilling your tank of creativity or building your creative community. These workshops can really help give you the boost of confidence that you really need if you are ever at a loss about how to get started on a project. Generally speaking, instructors hand out all materials and guide you through everything, step by step, so you don't need to worry about making a mistake and wasting the materials, which are all part of the learning process.

I can vouch for the regenerative nature of such workshops from my personal experience. An event that will stay with me for a lifetime was a *"Creative Reuse in Home Décor"* workshop conducted at a local arts center. It was working on old fabrics and garments to make something new and fresh. Though a bit intimidating at first, I was enthusiastic about entering the textile sector. The workshop was facilitated by a well-known local artist. We learned how to make our own colorful tapestries out of fabric scraps, old clothes, and mismatched buttons. Of course, it was quite overwhelming in the beginning, but somewhere down the line, I found my place as the artist started leading us on color choices, sewing techniques, and design basics. It was quite a collaborative atmosphere where everyone learned from each other. After the workshop, I had a not-so-quiet tapestry and valuable insights on where to source affordable materials for future projects. The thrift stores and fabric shops were the game-changers for those fabric scraps that are really cheap, so I could, from that point onwards, sustain my crafting ideas without really breaking the bank.

What it really birthed was ***confidence***. Talking to other people, asking questions, and sharing my ideas not only helped me perfect my crafts but also dramatically improved my ability to relate with other people. This extended beyond crafting and began to affect almost every part of my life, from sourcing materials in markets to talking to my neighbors about zero-waste. So, see what workshops are available in your area. More than likely, your local community center or library has information on this subject as promotion flyers or newsletters at the front desk of the building for upcoming events. Just jump in and join! Whether it's weaving, soldering, or maybe even sculpting, each new skill will take you toward realizing all of your zero-waste dreams. Remember, every creation helps to bring a better community with sustainable lives to fruition.

Embracing the Hunt as Part of the Adventure

Isn't there an exciting allure to a treasure hunt? This is basically the feeling you get in the scavenger hunt for upcycling material—excitement. Every time you set off in search of the hidden treasures for your projects, you embark on a small expedition. The thrill is in the randomness of what you are likely to come across. Consider each flea market, yard sale, and thrift store as the way leading to buried treasures—the way pirates used to be. Each might bring its own surprise along the way, like an old, tattered wooden frame to be used for a rural-style mirror or a bunch of old postcards to be used in a photo collage. Full of surprises and teachings, just like a good adventure. Even more charming is the fact that these things are not collected to own them but rather to go on a treasure hunt for the stories behind them. Maybe that teapot with a chipped rim once graced the table of some long-ago newlywed, or those leather belts destined for the discount bin were once lovingly hand-tooled by some far-off artisan. As you gather those items, you don't amass materials but anecdotes and creative inspiration.

And what about all the people that you run into during this adventure? Speaking to the vendors about the history of an item or with other crafters about project ideas can bring so much more into an experience. Sometimes, these conversations will segue into tips on other places to explore or even offers of future collaborations.

So why not put it into gear and start your creating in earnest with a scavenger hunt? Alone or with a pal for the adventure, bring with you a bag for all your finds and your imagination. Stroll through busy markets or browse garage sales; meander through neighborhoods filled with yard sales. Not only will every trip re-supply your project arsenal, but each expedition will further develop your powers of perception and your ability to see the beauty in the trash. Remember, each saved and upcycled item makes the world a tad more magical in terms of eco-friendliness. You are not just making art; you are making a difference. So, get the feeling of the hunt and the adventure, and let every find inspire you, ignite your creativity and curiosity to know more.

My Personal Journey in Material Sourcing

What were the first things you did when you started zero-waste? Well, the first project I did for zero-waste was a headboard out of an old wooden door. The project wasn't great, but it was personal and told a story. With that success under my belt, I started to look around for the next materials that might be ripe for a change. I distinctly remember making a vintage-style wall clock out of a few old vinyl records. As I became braver, my discoveries expanded to how I could interact with local businesses. One of my treasured discoveries was a cache of expired wallpaper books acquired from a local decorator. With a little imagination, I was able to transform those gorgeous pages into interesting wall art and lovely gift wraps.

"Looking Forward"

Now that I am continuing down this path, sourcing materials comes naturally to me. Before throwing something away, I naturally think of how it could be re-used. This hasn't just changed my frame of mind to reduce my waste output, but it has made my living space unique with the one-of-a-kind decor that tells its own stories.

Encouragement for Your Own Journey

I encourage you to take this journey of discovery for yourself. For now, just start by looking around the house and outdoors. What are all the things that are within reach for you? How can they be changed or put to another use? Get started on the little, easily doable ways, and then allow yourself to try them out. Success builds more confidence and leads to better skills.

It is more than just home decor—this sourcing and gathering adventure is about reshaping your relationship with the world. It is an odyssey toward sustainable living, an appreciation for the richness that surrounds you, and cultivating beauty from the overlooked and mundane. So, put that bag on your shoulder and your explorer cap on your head, and step into the creative world of sourcing. It's amazing what comes out of the woodwork, and then, of course, these benefits accrue to you, not only you but also your household and the environment. Let's make this an adventure worth remembering!

Storing and Organizing Materials

So, now that you've prepped on where to source materials for your projects, here is the next most important step: ordering. This is not just about sourcing the perfect pieces; it's the process of order that allows one's creative juices to flow smoothly. That transition from scattered potential to a well-ordered toolkit: ***it's really the stuff of magic***.

Treat your workspace like a chef treats their kitchen: everything has a place, and each thing is in its place. This will streamline your creative process and make it enjoyable. This has nothing to do with big spaces or expensive storage solutions; it's just all about making the most of what you have and turning the idea of organization into a creative pursuit.

First of all, set aside some area in your house to do your crafting. It need not be something big; maybe a corner of your room or even your garage. Shelving units are truly helpful for those bulkier items, whereas smaller containers or jars work great to house those easily misplaced materials.

Labeling is your friend in this venture. Think about it: quickly finding the right necklace or material bits without having to dig through every box. Quick labeling saves time and keeps you in the creative flow.

Following the spirit of zero-waste, even materials can be reused in storage solutions. This can range from using old jars for buttons or screws to using larger ones for fabrics or papers and even using decorated shoeboxes for smaller crafting tools.

Don't forget to look up! Your walls can be more than just the final resting place for your completed projects; pegboards, magnetic boards, and hooks can make unclaimed wall space purposeful and decorative wall space. This not only keeps your materials handy but turns them into a part of the room's decor.

Proper storage also ensures that the materials last for a long period of time. For instance, keeping fabric out of the sun will prevent it from fading. The same goes for paper—keeping it from getting wet will prevent it from warping. This careful handling is going to pay off so much because you will have them in good condition when the time comes for them to be used in the next project.

Well, it was a struggle for me in the beginning. I got so frustrated because my stuff was everywhere, and I would use things up. That's when I made a pledge to organize, even if it was putting a label on boxes at first. Over time, it worked out well. I developed a system that maximized the floor space in my tiny studio apartment. Now, my craft area is inspiring. An organized space breeds the excitement of new projects, not intimidation. Making an effort to organize your space is an investment in future creativity.

Build your crafting space slowly over time. Organize by type of material, one type at a time, until you have fine-tuned your system. Time establishes a natural rhythm toward a greater, creative, and productive process. This is not just an aesthetic exercise; it nurtures a milieu for growth, thereby making every crafting experience more enjoyable and productive. In fact, such a systematic approach might even go beyond the sphere of crafting and be applied to other walks of life.

Take the next step, organize your materials, and watch your crafting space — and creativity — flourish!

Safety First

Now that you have sorted and arranged all these materials, next is safety. Preparation for the handling and reuse of materials is crucial not only to make the product attractive but, above all, to do so in a safe manner. This step is vital, ensuring that your crafting projects will be both safe and secure while also being lots of fun. When you are recycling materials, especially those not intended for crafting, safe handling is crucial to make sure that your project comes out with panache. This is a concern for you and for the end result. Safety can be part of your crafting routine to make sure that each project turns out as a winner, not only through your eyes but by structure as well.

First things first, you have to consider the nature of what you are handling. For example, if you have a project that requires the cutting of glass bottles to use as a vase or a candle holder, then you have to use the right material that is needed to get the job done. You may need to use a glass cutter; hence, you should make sure that you safeguard yourself from the dangers of the material by having on gloves and the right protective eye gear. Since glass is unpredictable when it shatters, it is important to learn how to score and snap glass safely.

Working with wood? Sure, sanding is no problem for old wood items, but watch out—old paint could have lead, particularly if it was manufactured prior to the 1970s. Health can be protected with just some basic precautions, such as wearing a mask to avoid breathing in dust and working in a well-ventilated area.

While the electrical components offer a few neat potentials, like an old bit of electronics to make a new lamp, it can be dangerous to work with the wiring if one is not careful about shocks or starting fires. You'll be set to go if you learn some basic electrical safety measures, how to make proper wire connections, and just how important proper grounding is—not like this.

Chemicals are a further worry. In all instances, use non-toxic alternatives when stripping paints or applying finishes, and do so in a well-ventilated area. The volatility of the chemicals may dictate that gloves and a respirator are necessary.

A clean and organized workplace cuts back on the risks of accidents immensely. Keep tools and materials stored safely, especially if you have pets or children. Neat workspaces reduce the chances of accidents happening from badly stored tools and make finding things easy.

These lessons are mostly learned the hard way, through personal experience. At the very initial stages of upcycling, I just plunged in without any knowledge, only enthusiasm. In the middle of a project on reclaimed wood, I became very uncomfortable because of the sanding dust. Later, I had a very harsh cough, and my eyes were itching a lot. From this experience, I learned that it is important to be well-prepared and to protect oneself with respiratory masks. Those experiences shaped my approach to DIY. I first give priority to researching and investing in protective gear to set up a safe workspace before embarking on any project. Such a proactive approach adds not only to the enjoyment but also to the item, giving it an aura of workmanship and care.

Safety first may feel like a step further, but it certainly is basic. It ensures that your crafting endeavors not only make your home more beautiful but also improve your well-being. After all, the goal is to be able to enjoy the creations fully without compromise. By prioritizing safety, you create an environment that values and protects your health in a way that handcrafted pieces are beautiful and carefully crafted. Spend some time getting to know your materials and finding out about safety features. It's that kind of precaution for which your future self and your projects will thank you. In crafting, just like in life, it's always better to err on the side of caution. It will make sure you are safe while creating and will make sure your handcrafted decor has integrity and longevity, proving to all that each piece is a showcase of creativity and careful craftsmanship.

CHAPTER 4

ZERO-WASTE PROJECTS FOR BEGINNERS

With Chapter 4, we really are taking the plunge now into creative, sustainable, and eco-friendly living. This chapter is all for people who are just starting out and want to see and do something really simple but impactful with the hope that it will just step them into the world of eco-crafting. Let's start upcycling old clothes into chic, no-sew fabric wraps to give a new life to the discarded textiles. We are going to upcycle glass jars into sweet little planters, so any place is filled with greenery and charm. Finally, see how to hand-make paper out of stuff that's been recycled so that everyday rubbish gets transformed into beautiful and useful artifacts. Complete with step-by-step directions, listed are all the tools and supplies needed and even some cool little tricks on how to make each of the projects your own, tailored to fit your specific style and preference. The projects are thus not just an easy and fun thing to do but a really great, low-stakes way for you to be introduced to the principles behind a truly fulfilling zero-waste lifestyle. So, let us unleash our creative side to bring beauty to something others would not even look at!

Project 1: No-Sew Fabric Wraps from Old Clothes

Have you ever looked in your wardrobe and seen those things

that you just can't throw away—no matter what the condition? Maybe it's that favorite t-shirt you've had for days and days or a dress that has had a favored print go out of fashion and is now in the back of the closet. Rather than hide these treasures, or worse yet, throw them away, why not resurrect them? So our first project is making no-sew cloth wraps out of old clothes; that way, you get to reduce waste and revitalize cherished garments.

Getting Started

Start this project by gathering a few basic tools and materials, most of which are likely to be found at your place, and thus make it a really good first project to embark on. Here's what you're going to need:

- ***Old Clothes***: Watch out for those textiles that are not very worn-out and are still relatively strong and pleasing aesthetically, like cotton T-shirts, flannel shirts, or even lightweight sweaters.
- ***Scissors***: A sharp pair will cut the fabric nicely.
- ***Ruler or Tape Measure***: These are useful for cutting out pieces to the size you want—precisely.
- ***Tailor's chalk or marker***: You use this to mark your cuts in advance of time.

It's a very simple project that allows a lot of customization, which is what makes it so cute. Here's how you can *get started*:

1. Prepare Your Fabric:

Lay your selected garment out on a flat surface. Level out any creases, and you are ready to do your cutting. If you work with a t-shirt, you might want to use the main body for larger wraps and the sleeves for smaller ones.

For me: I made the project using an old flannel shirt that belonged to my grandfather. It was well worn through at the elbows and had quite a bit of fading, but there is no doubt about the sentimental value that the plaid pattern brings. I spread that across my dining table, making sure to pull out any wrinkles in the fabric. This very initial step of preparation not only assisted in the cutting process but also allowed me to ponder the memories associated with the material.

2. Measure and Mark:

Choose your wrap size. One typical starting size would be roughly 12 x 12 inches. With a ruler and some fabric chalk, carefully measure and mark your cut lines. Note that you can always change your dimensions to fit your style or the size of the remnant you have on hand.

For me: I took a measuring tape with me and found some 12x12-inch wraps—the perfect size for small presents. Taking the time to measure carefully and mark the shirt with fabric chalk, I realized my lines were crooked in the first go, so that was a good lesson. This was the step I kind of liked because I had to try and fit the most interesting parts of the plaid pattern into the squares I'd drawn.

3. Cut Your Fabric:

Cut your fabric squares, following the markings you have just made. Expect a little fraying along the edges; it will only add to the rustic charm of these fabric wraps. If fraying isn't really your thing, you can seal the edges with a thin application of clear fabric glue.

For me: But as soon as I was about to cut that fabric, the expectations went up in my head. Following the chalk lines with my sharp scissors, I was reforming an old shirt into several square parts. The first snip was very liberating, and I almost felt like I was doing something forbidden by cutting an old piece of clothing. As each cut followed, I gained more and more confidence as the fabric took on a new role, assuming a new identity and purpose before my eyes.

4. Wrap it Up:

You have cut the fabric, and now your wraps are good to go! Wrap gifts, use them as napkins, or use them as little bags to carry household items.

For me: When all of the pieces were finally trimmed, I was left with a stack of very finely detailed squares of fabric. I folded one into a triangle and wrapped it around a book that was to be given away, tied it up with a piece of twine again, and the fraying gave it a nice but not too much over-the-top touch. I also ran a drop of clear fabric glue along one on a different piece to arrest any more fraying on that one as well, and that worked just great while holding the hand of the fabric.

Last but not least, one after the other of these steps, the shirt of my grandfather was all in one piece, both functional and aesthetically nice. Every wrap bears the essence of the life led before and the marks of my crafting journey. This taught me satisfaction and fulfillment from crafting with my own hands.

Customizing Your Fabric Wraps

Now you know the basic technique, let's learn how to make these wraps your own. Here are some ideas:

1. Mix and Match:

Scavenge for different fabrics from different clothes and do a patchwork wrap. This will not only be of visual interest but will also allow for the adjustment of sizes if needed.

For me: As I got bolder with my fabric wraps, I decided to mess around with mixing them up. I found a few old T-shirts and denim remnants from jeans that were long gone. Cutting them into strips, I laid them all out on my living room floor like some sort of crafty, cozy puzzle. I didn't even stitch them up, just a little dab of fabric glue. Voilà!

The contrast between the softness of the cotton and the rigidity of the denim was great for wrapping items like books or even a set of DIY tools.

2. Add Decorations:

Personalize your wraps more with fabric paint, iron-on decals, or embroidery. It can even be a fun activity for kids.

For me: And now, the fun part—decorating. I made a wrap for a friend who loves gardening. I selected green material and decorated the wrap with tiny flowers by painting them on with fabric paint. Although I am far from an artist, the wrap took on a special look with my homemade designs. On another occasion, I decorated a wrap with a happy iron-on decal. This is all it really needed to have a fresh feeling of fun. These decorations converted the wraps from mere pieces of cloth to miniature works of art.

3. Functional Additions:

Add buttons, ties, or Velcro that would close and keep the wraps in place, making them more functional, especially if you foresee this project to be used multiple times as gift wrap.

For me: Adding functional details, such as ties or Velcro, was a complete game changer. I have stitched a few ties from the remaining fabric into a wrap, and as it were, I had just made some bread, which I intended to give to my neighbor. It fastened the bundle right up. Another time, I sewed Velcro tabs on the sides of a wrap that I was using to keep my charging cables together while not in use in the house. The result was pretty darn useful and could easily be used over and over again.

Every one of those steps is aimed at working with the visual aesthetics of the wraps while making them as effective as possible for you. Whether these additions are for visual appeal or adding functionality, these all pay off incredibly in what is achieved using these ordinary pieces of fabric. It's really quite amazing what you can do with just a little creative inspiration and a couple of old garments, isn't it?

The Impact of Your Effort & A Personal Touch

Then follows the sense of your effort and the personal connection.

As I began this no-sew fabric wrap project, it was very much like paging through an old photo album—each piece of fabric holding its own story. For instance, cutting into my grandpa's old, worn flannel shirt brought with it a mix of nostalgia and anticipation: There is something just a bit bold in taking what you are so familiar with and transforming it into something utterly fresh and vital. And soon, this became the therapeutic activity of making those wraps really fast. It was very satisfying to give the old clothes a new life. More than saving the planet, one piece of fabric at a time, it was a journey of feeling reconnected to the cherished memories given a new lease of life. And there is no way that one is not satisfied when something absolutely beautiful is created out of things marked for garbage.

Giving these wraps as gifts? Pure hit! My friends and family really liked them, not only because of the looks but for the stories behind them. It's pretty cool how a simple piece of fabric can hold so much meaning and become a conversation starter.

This project had an epiphany itself: small acts, like the reuse of the old fabric, create a great impact. This is about seeing the potential in the most ordinary things. Those shirts thrown away are no longer just shirts; they are new businesses, new ornamentations just waiting to come alive.

Engaging in this type of crafting has really opened my eyes to what can be upcycled. I have always been in thought, *"What can I do with a new piece?"*. It goes far, far, far further than just being environmentally friendly—it is making it something unique and personal. There is really no happiness like this: creating wonders from something that was just an ordinary possession!

"Looking Forward"

Congratulations on completing your first project! There's nothing like that first moment of pulling up in real life what you've made. Since you've just taken your first baby steps in the magical realm of creation, are you ready to kick it up a notch? Your house is a treasure trove of hidden potential—those old jeans, that dusty curtain, or even those odd socks could be your next project superstar. Think of it as a wonderful treasure hunt, where every piece promises to save and change the rescued. The fulfillment after completion of those projects is so satisfying, right? You are now beginning a journey of real change—not only in improving the living environment but also in developing a lifestyle of a greener shade. So, what's next on your creativity list? Maybe those piles of old magazines could become a dynamic collage, or those bits and pieces of yarn could be turned into a cozy throw. Each project builds on the other, which builds your skills and imagination. Let's keep this creative adventure going and see the endless places our creativity can go!

Project 2: Décorative Glass Jar Planters

Now, it's time to up your game of repurposing even more. Let's dive into our next project. Sweet little plain glass jars, kept in the back of your cupboards—now cute little decorative planters. Thanks to the wraps project, you are a pro at repurposing, so it is time to add a dash of green to your space.

Gathering Your Materials

To get started with this, you're going to need all those glass jars you've been saving. They can be old mason jars, upcycled pickle containers—whatever you want them to be. You'll also need:

- Acrylic paint or glass markers for decoration
- Potting soil
- Miniature plants or succulents
- Gravels for drainage
- Ornamental qualities may include twine, shells, or beads

Prepping Your Jars

Start by cleaning your jars thoroughly to remove any labels and sticky residue. A soak in warm, soapy water usually does the trick, while stubborn glue spots can be tackled with a touch of rubbing alcohol. Once squeaky clean and dry, it's time to embark on their makeover.

"Personal Experience"

When I started making planters from glass jars, my kitchen was filled with them, from repurposed spaghetti sauce containers to sweet jelly jars salvaged from my morning toast. The first step in the process was to prepare the jars; it was something like priming a canvas before painting. I started running warm, soapy water into the kitchen sink as I filled the jars. The labels became loose, and with very little effort, I was able to pull them off while the jars soaked in the water. There were a few labels so strong that they didn't want to leave the surface of the glass. In that case, a drop of olive oil was priceless, taking away the glue residue without spoiling the surface of the glass. There were a few jars that appeared to be cloudy after all the labels had been removed. I scrubbed those with a soft sponge and rinsed well, clearing them of all the remnants with rubbing alcohol. As the jars sat drying on the counter, basking in the full sunlight, I simply felt great. All these tiny glass containers that had been thrown away were now ready to be transformed into beautiful home decor objects. Unexpectedly, preparing the jars was pleasurable. It felt like a first step towards their transformation, and getting it right felt like a key to setting the stage for the creative steps to follow.

Getting Creative with Decorating

This is where your imagination goes wild! If you decide on painting, consider if you are one who enjoys a plain color or something a little fancier. For instance, stripes, polka dots, or even the latest ombre effect can really show off some pizzazz. Going to go with glass markers? Think about drawing fancy designs or inscribing fabulous quotes directly on the glass.

"Personal Experience"

The first one was kind of coastal. I painted them in sandy beige and ocean blue, then accented the tops with twine and added the small seashells that I had collected from beach outings. They reminded me of sunny days at the beach and made me feel so carefree.

Planting Your Greenery

After your jars have been decorated and the paint is dry, it is now time to start setting up a good environment for your green buddies. Line the bottom with a few pebbles of each jar to assist in the draining process—useful for the healthy lives of the plants that you put in. Fill them in with potting soil, and carefully nestle your chosen plants or succulents into their new abodes. Succulents, on the other hand, are very manageable; they don't require much watering or caring for.

"Personal Experience"

The rush of excitement in preparing to plant my greenery in the newly painted jars bordered an almost imperceptible feeling of nervousness. Each one of them was now a miniature garden, and I was to take care of them. Going with succulents of many types seemed appropriate since they are sturdy and hardy, just like me, and sometimes, I end up with situations in my life.

I put a layer of little pebbles in the bottom of each jar. Besides being pleasing to the eye, it allows for proper drainage, which is very important for developing healthy succulent roots. Spooning in the already-moistened potting soil was a welcome mat for the plants. It was like adding the last pieces of a living puzzle. I ran my finger through the soil, barely making an indentation, before lifting out the succulents from their nursery pots. I cradled the succulents in my hands, spreading the roots a little, and then placed them in their new beds for a snug but comfortable fit.

Once all the plants were accommodated, a final layer of pebbles was added over the soil, holding the design in stabilization and preventing the pooling of water—succulents abhor stagnant water. Stepping back for a moment, I looked at my handiwork and really felt this strong connection to the verdant lives now encased in my creations. It was a feeling that transcended mere crafting; it was a sense of a small act of ingenuity. Water seeped through the pebbles and soil as I was watering them for the first time, straight to their roots. It washed over me: a sense of relief that I had given my green friends the very best possible beginning in their new home. All those days of careful work have gone into making their new home. Now, every time I mist them, as I did, you see, it means something more. Witnessing their blooming growth imparts me with satisfaction, and it leads to my home feeling filled with peace and nature.

Positioning Your Planters

Think about where your new pots will work best: A sunny windowsill, a central table, or even a bathroom counter will be ideal. They do require light, but most succulents prefer plenty of indirect sunlight, so there's no need to worry if your place is not too sunny.

"Personal Experience"

Once I had potted my new succulent friends, after doing my best to take good care of them and put them into an appropriately sized pot, it was time to put them in their rightful place among my home's living spaces. It felt almost as though I were creating mini-displays around my house. I started in the kitchen, which is a great spot for plants that like bright, indirect light, with the early sun pouring over the countertop at the sink. I hung three of the jar planters I had just designed, and the fresh green colors and earthy tones really shined out against the otherwise pure white of the kitchen walls. Walking through the entrance, the living room has dimmer lighting, with just the right corner for reading and a jar containing a couple of succulents that don't mind the shade coming from the bookcase. The refreshing life of such decorative features is brought among the realm of the literary and beloved photographs, complementing the ambiance of the space.

Embracing creativity, my exploration of botany extended to the bathroom with a small planter on a window ledge. The gentle humidity seeping from the shower offered a promise of much-needed nourishment to the succulent while taking this room to the level of a sanctuary I find much the same as a spa retreat. I've planted them all in specific places, not only for their benefit but also for what they bring to the room. Now and again, I would rearrange them so all the plants get an equal amount of light and refresh the feel of the room. All these little accents do make a difference in my home's feel. They become more than just botanicals; they develop into dynamic elements of a living work of art that breathes life and personality into every corner they occupy.

Customization Tips

For real individuality, you could tie on colored ribbons around the jars or add custom tags with plant names or care instructions in some fancy calligraphy. It's those personalized touches that make your creations one of a kind.

"Personal Experience"

When I set off on the personalization journey, that's truly when the fun began in my crafting experience. I loved being able to add those little touches that made every planter unique. However, one of my personal customization favorites is the addition of natural jute twine. Wrapping the jute around the rim of the jars and securing them with a touch of hot glue added a rustic charm while making the planter easy to hold in.

So, I played around with color in my own experiments. I did up some jars in bright, multi-color beads and little charms and then set them off against the green background of the succulents, with a lot of colors, to pop some life into the settings. It was like each jar was speaking with a different voice. For an added touch of class—especially to those I intended to put in my sitting room—I used metallic paint to trace out intricate gold and silver designs on the jars. This discreet decoration gave them more than enough chic to fit right in with the rest of the room's decor.

I also made my own labels for the jars: dainty wooden tags with the names of the plants carefully written out in calligraphy and hung from the jar necks with little leather strings. The labels were in place not just as devices for caring for the plant but also for sophistication, like those in high botanical presentations. These personal touches went beyond aesthetics and further created a connection and pride in the project. Every look at the planters speaks of much more than just plants in glass; they stand for a collection of meticulously prepared art pieces, together with my personal touch and special meaning within my home.

Seeing the Results

Seeing the plants thrive in the decorative containers is just so satisfying. It is a physical example of all of the work and creativity that you have done. The other thing is just what these botanical decorations do in terms of adding life and personalization to your space; truly, very few experiences compare with this one in terms of how rewarding it can be to add nature to your home environment through your very own efforts.

"Personal Experience"

Seeing all those flourishing glass jar planters around my house has been an overwhelmingly rewarding experience. Okay, so I take quite a bit of aesthetic pleasure in those little succulents growing in their tiny pots, but more so in the feeling of great contentment that I had been instrumental in giving them these darling little new homes. Every morning, when I do my usual routine of brewing coffee, I take a minute to look at the green inhabitants out my kitchen window. Dappled with the soft light of the morning sun and their leaves shining, one can sense a current of great fulfillment and peace.

One of the cutest examples was when the new shoots started to come up a few weeks after I planted that brilliant succulent in the pot with the azulé and ivory stripes. I glanced over to see that new shoots were already coming up, a very subtle yet definite omen of its happiness in this place of nurturing. Such sprouting not only reflected my green thumb but also the nurturing place that the planter was. Equally satisfying were the comments from friends and family who visited. They were immediately drawn to the quirky pots with questions galore and comments that were over the top in appreciation for the creativity of the designs. And it was so much fun to be able to share the stories behind each pot—the choices of embellishments, selections of plants, and even their placements. Other conversations had to do with reflections on ways that items might be upcycled in their own homes.

Apart from that, the planters played a dominating role in other spaces as well, which made a living impression that might assist in rejuvenating the atmosphere through a rainbow of colors. Be it snuggled within the sitting-room corner or decked out on the lighted kitchen countertop, each and every planter carries the power of adding a new dimension of decoration that is pleasing to the eyes. It was very fulfilling to see material results not only from the planters but also from the atmosphere they had created in my home. It reminded me that, with some touch of creativity and work input, even ordinary things can turn into a source of aesthetic pleasure and fullness of emotions.

"Looking Ahead"

From then on, after the very first experiment with planters, it was not to be taken back. From being just a nice gift to friends, very soon, interest in my work has blown up. Each pot was a fresh new canvas, and with each new project, I fell more in love with crafting. It was becoming something more than just a hobby—it was starting to be the way in which I could express myself in my own living space and in that of others.

So, why not start with your own? With a bit of elbow grease and a dash of creativity, you will be amazed at how much pleasure it can be to turn ordinary jars into beautiful working pieces of art. Believe me, it is a journey you will identify with, and it will enhance your soul and the surroundings. Let's continue with this crafting odyssey; there's a universe full of creativity waiting for our exploration!

Project 3: Handmade Paper from Scrap Paper

After your glass jar planters are made, imagine how much more satisfying it will be to work on another project. Let's get down and dirty on the following: how to make recycled handmade paper out of trash scrap. Not only is this a very cool thing to do with those paper bits that tend to end up in the trash, but it also produces nice green paper for decorating all sorts of things.

Gathering Your Materials

To start off with, we grab the fundamentals:

- Scratch paper: You can gather a mix of old newspapers, invoices, correspondence, or whatever other loose papers you can find.
- A large basin or tub
- Blender
- A-frame or an old picture frame with a screen
- A sponge
- A piece of felt or a fabric scrap
- A rolling pin (optional for extra smoothness)

Prepping Your Paper

Begin by shredding your waste paper into tiny pieces about the size of a postage stamp. This will make further processing and conversion to pulp much easier. Fill your blender about half full with lukewarm water; then add the shredded paper pieces and blend until you have a smooth, thick solution. There! That's the basic material for your new paper project.

For me: Starting my journey into papermaking, I discovered a treasure trove of scrap paper lying hidden in my house: old bills, newspapers, and various other notes, waiting for their metamorphosis from wasted remains into works of art. The very first step of the entire process was to tear these pieces into tiny, stamp-sized pieces, symbolically relieving the old to allow something new and magnificent to take its place. Lever adjusted to the right consistency, it is nested into a bath of warm water and roared into life, setting the scraps almost into a trancing transformation. The once-disjointed scraps merged into a luscious, pulpy concoction, such that one could not easily tell from where the pieces had originated; a perfect example of the transmutation of creativity. I could be an alchemist at that very moment, turning the mundane into the extraordinary.

Forming the Paper

Ladle the pulp into a basin that already has some extra warm water in it. The excess water will help lift the pulp onto your frame more evenly. Lower the screen of your frame into the basin, collect some of the pulp, and bring it up. Let the surplus water drain back into the basin—not a bad beginning for your baby paper sheet.

For me: So, after I was done with my pulp, I was now supposed to actually form the paper sheets; it almost felt like the heart of the craft. I just poured the pulp mixture into more water in a large basin. This diluted mixture helped the fibers to float, making it easier to form sheets. I then used an upcycled picture frame with a piece of mesh screen fitted inside and dunked it into the basin. Using a slow, gentle upward motion, I lifted the suspended pulp. Upon bringing the frame up, a gentle waterfall began to flow down, leaving a fine layer of pulp on the screen. It was always a sort of magic to watch how the water retreated and revealed the gradual movement of the fibers coming together into a unified sheet. I attempted to keep my hand as still as could be on the frame; then, I added the most subtle of lateral rocking movements. This rocking helped the pulp spread fairly even over the screen in both thickness and texture so that the resulting paper would be uniform. Great precision was involved: if it were rocked too much, there would be thinning in different areas, or if it was not rocked enough, there could be some clumping. Frankly, from the very beginning, the attempts had been far from perfect, as uneven thicknesses and frayed edges had marred the result. However, with every new try, I got closer and closer to the idiosyncrasies of pulp behavior. Each batch, really, was one step forward, and with it, every sheet was a small victory. This tactile engagement with the paper-making process proved profoundly fulfilling, offering tangible evidence of metamorphosis unfolding before my very eyes.

Drying the Paper

Spread the pulp onto the screen and lightly squeeze the pulp with a sponge by pushing it down, which will soak up some of the excess water and press the fibers together. Then, lift the screen carefully and turn the wet sheet of paper over onto a piece of felt. Light tapping might be needed to get the paper to release. Using a rolling pin, carefully roll on top of the paper to even it out and remove any extra moisture.

For me: The next challenge was making sure that the sheet dries well after finishing the paper forming. Initially, I used to place the wet paper sheets on a level surface covered with absorbent cloths and towels. Systematically, I added some pressure on it by using another towel. This way, extra moisture is sucked out of the sheet. That was quite a delicate process, as too much force could rip the paper, whereas too little would not allow the paper to dry.

Finally, the moment of truth was when the screen was blotted off. There was, to be sure, always a little bit of tension at this point, at least the first couple of times. I carefully lifted an edge, taking the paper onto a piece of felt. The absorbent felt allowed to mop moisture up and also promoted airflow around the paper, which helped the even drying. Sometimes, with an added piece of felt, which is sometimes topped by a light book for pressure, the result was just to keep the paper as flat as possible during drying since moisture in the paper sought to move and escape the sheet. The paper dried with almost no curl at the edge. The slow change from wet pulp to a strong sheet was really a rewarding experience. It takes a whole day, or even longer, for it to dry completely, depending on the thickness and the humidity in the air.

As the papers dried, I peeped at them from time to time and felt a combination of excitement and satisfaction. Each sheet that dried correctly confirmed that the time and effort were well worth it and that it was vastly satisfying to create something real and functional out of just scraps. Even if time-consuming, this was an excellent reminder of the beauty and potential that recycled materials already house within them.

Decorating Your Paper

This is where you can add personality to your paper. While it is still moist, sprinkle some dried flowers, petite leaves, and even a dash of glitter on the surface. Gently press these embellishments into the pulp, and voilà. Each adds a distinct texture and visual appeal to your final creation.

For me: As soon as the paper sheets had dried enough to be just damp, I moved to the stage of decoration. This was always so much fun, creating works of art that were one of a kind using ordinary sheets. I sprinkled some dried flowers and leaves on a few of them, pressing them gently into the pulp. These flowers and leaves, with their varied colors and shapes, gave the sheets a very pretty look and, in fact, a texture; every sheet was different and interesting.

For a more playful look, especially for the paper that I intended to use for crafting with nieces and nephews. I sometimes add just a little glitter or small colored paper fragments left over from other projects. If I do that, I use a very light touch and drop them onto the paper when it is still very wet so that they blend into the paper without disrupting the structure of the pulp.

The one I remember most was what I was trying to make into a themed stationery set. I added a few drops of essential oil to the pulp for a light scent and stamped the paper before it fully dried to embed the design. The whole time, I remember, it required such a gentle but confident touch: push too hard, and the paper would tear; press too lightly, and the design wouldn't stick. The embellishment phase went further than just aesthetics: it would be taken into thoughtful consideration if this paper will be for letter writing, gift-wrapping, or journaling. Thus, each action done in this phase was purposely designed to make the handmade paper utilitarian, filled with intention and individuality.

Drying and Using Your Handmade Paper

Allow the paper to dry completely; it usually takes a day or two, depending on the thickness of the paper and the humidity level. Use the dried handmade paper for a multitude of uses: to make greeting cards, bookmarks, or even frames as unique artwork.

For me: After the embellishment step, the pages needed to be completely dried, something that took my patience away. I found the best way was to lay them flat in a well-aired room and out of direct sunlight to avoid all kinds of distortion and color loss. I soon invented a sort of drying rack out of old window screens, which helped a lot in getting air to move around each page. Eventually, it made the process of drying quicker, all while keeping the paper's texture. That, indeed, was a magical transformation underway with the drying. It started out as a wet mess of pulp but slowly took on strength and texture into a sheet still bearing the impressions of flowers and leaves or whatever other decoration I had selected. It was like watching watercolor paintings come alive, with each sheet being different—capturing a momentary moment in time. The use of this paper, when dried, was satisfaction at its peak. I still remember the first time I wrote a letter to a friend using this paper. The roughness in its texture through my hands made it a different experience altogether. It was as if I was giving away a part of myself in the process of writing.

Over time, I would use the paper for a variety of projects: greeting cards, bookmarks, and decorating book covers—the thrill of satisfaction with every use. Eventually, I started giving pieces of my handmade paper away with an explanation of the process written on a card. Friends and family always marveled at the time and care that went into every sheet. The process of drying and the handmade paper taught me a lot of patience and the satisfaction that comes from being able to shepherd a project from inception to completion. It was almost as though each new batch of paper gave way to a poignant reminder of the fact that new and brilliant utilitarian creations could be born out of a small, repurposed material with a sprinkle of creativity and the abundant sincerity that one can muster.

Reflecting on the Journey

Engaging in the process of transforming these wastes into paper goes beyond DIY; it is a small but remarkable step toward sustainability. More than old scraps turned into new, novel, and attractive forms, it changes the way I see waste, triggering creativity in ways unexplored before. I shall always recall the peaceful nights spent sifting through newly made piles of paper, for each piece had a story of its own. I understood that this was something more than just a hobby for me; it turned out to be a part of my life and a physically expressive mechanism of my commitment to zero waste.

Every step of the way, from working with remnants of old paper to foliage and petals, has instilled in me an ethos of mindfulness, which encourages an extremely careful deceleration in order to relish life's minutiae. It took me much time and experience to steer through the mishaps and revel in the triumphs to realize that I have grown in the process. The mishaps, from a messed-up batch to the initial struggle to acquire the perfect consistency of pulp, have been building forces for both resilience and adaptability. And when my efforts were rewarded with success, the gratification was beyond words! It was not just paper-making; it was the growth that was symbolic, one sheet of paper at a time.

This started many eye-opening conversations about recycling, creativity, and the effects of our daily decisions. It warmed my soul to see the interest it had created in my family and social circles in making their own paper or even rethinking their consumption habits.

Looking back, I don't have words to express what all the learning in the paper-making process has added to life. It is more than a craft—it is a means by which one can develop a community, raise environmental consciousness, be creative, and be an environmental steward. Each and every batch of paper is a reminder, a modest but important example, of how we might each contribute to a better world—one beautiful sheet at a time.

"Looking Ahead"

Since the inception of my paper-making experiments, I've employed multiple textures and augmentations; each batch is a journey into experimentation, and each result brings satisfaction. Sharing these creations brings personal satisfaction and joy to my loved ones, who often get handmade, bespoke cards from my handmade paper. *Why shouldn't you set out on that journey?* This very well can be your new passion, to take away waste yet at the same time produce such really beautiful works that are very useful. It's a rewarding, fun activity that benefits not just personally but also through community and environmental means. Let's continue making beauty and art, one sheet at a time.

CHAPTER 5

FUNCTIONAL ZERO-WASTE PROJECTS

Now, in Chapter 5, let us see how some creative and practical solutions could add value and style to your functional living space. This chapter presents functional, aesthetic, and simple ways that turn ordinary items into an indispensable part of your home decor. We'll take you through creating bottle soap dispensers, a spice rack from reclaimed wood, and useful drawer organizers from old denim. Each project has clear, step-by-step instructions, detailed lists of what you'll need in terms of materials or tools, and insightful suggestions for customization in order to be able to tailor each piece to your space and your taste perfectly. Whether you are an experienced craftsman or new to the trade, all these projects have been designed with the purpose of helping you to bestow the gift of practicality and personality on your home, all while paying special attention to issues of sustainability.

Project 4: Upcycled Bottle Soap Dispensers

You won't know what kind of pride you feel inside when you see those you've managed to put together and know the end products are not just useful and beautiful but eco-friendly. So, let this not only be about good looks—this Upcycled Bottle Soap Dispensers but is safe in the choice of materials. Now, after you rolled up your sleeves and actually worked on those no-sew fabric wraps, the pretty glass jar planters, and handmade paper, you're looking at a different home—a home remade by your creativity and resourcefulness. And so, does it not give you a good feeling, that surge of pride, when you see those you've managed to put together, and you know that the end products are not only useful and beautiful but also eco-friendly?

Transforming Everyday Objects

So why soap dispensers, of all things? Think of it: all the many plastic bottles of soap that you buy and just throw in the garbage without another thought, yet each one of those is adding to the growing waste problem. But with a little creative thought and a tiny bit of work, you can make them into classy upcycled dispensers to help bring a bit of that stylized touch into your bathroom or kitchen.

Getting Started

- First off, get your materials in place. You will need:
- Empty glass bottles—wine or liquor bottles would work well for this.
- Soap pump—upcycle from an old dispenser or buy a new one.
- Glass drill with a special drill bit (according to the size of the pump).
- Safety goggles and gloves for protection.
- Waterproof sealant or high-grade adhesive

Step-by-Step Instructions

- ***Prepare the Bottle***: Clean the bottle well. Soak off any labels in warm, soapy water; they come off quite easily. Make sure the bottle is totally dry.
- ***Drilling the Hole***: With safety goggles and gloves in hand, drill a hole in the cap of the bottle or cork at a size that fits the soap pump. Do it slowly so that it doesn't crack, as this is a very important part of the project.
- ***Fitting the Pump***: Carefully push the pump into the hole. Using waterproof sealant or rigid glue, apply around the base of the pump where it meets the hole, sealing any leak.
- ***Finishing Touches***: Fill the remainder of the bottle with your favorite liquid soap. You can also add some of your favorite essential oils or soap colors from nature.

Customization Tips

- ***Personalize with Paint***: Enter the realm of glass paints and color your bottle using paints on the exterior surface. This dispenser could be the best centerpiece ever, be it in flowers, abstract art, or even some simple geometric design.
- ***Add Labels***: Make the waterproof labels with the initials of your family or the scent of the soap. This will make it look professional and assist in distinguishing the soap by type from others.
- ***Decorative Elements***: Decorate the neck of the bottle with a little twine or ribbon for that country look, or a little glam with some charms and beads.

Safety Alert! As in all things glass, be sure you are working in a safe place and have the proper protective gear on. Keep your workspace clean to avoid accidents, and if you're not comfortable drilling, practice on a piece of scrap glass first.

While you're doing this, you're going to put the new upcycled soap dispenser where it belongs by the sink. Look at your work. It's not just a soap dispenser; it's an example of the heart, soul, creativity, and mind of sustainability. You can use the fact of a step being taken right from the small steps, right through the tangible change made through this zero-waste journey.

Personal Experience

For my early crafting projects, I made a dozen of these for real, nice housewarming gifts.

Among all the upcycling projects, transforming old wine bottles into soap dispensers resonated with me the most. I undertook this project not because of recycling potential but because I was so enthused by the whole idea of sustainability. I hand-picked single bottles, each one to their shape and appeal. So, in that sense, the cleaning was a bit tedious, but once I saw the shiny bottles prepared to be reused, it was all worth it. It took a bit of a steady hand and patience to make the exact holes for the soap pumps. I really did enjoy it, especially once I found the pumps that matched the aesthetic of the bottles perfectly. I made personal touches with the mugs by using waterproof paint, while some are sleek and minimalistic, depending on the preference of my friends. Simple custom labels always bring a smile to new homeowners' faces when they read them.

It was such a great feeling to pack every dispenser into an eco-package and come to the housewarming party. It really felt warm inside seeing my friends open them with real appreciation and discuss recycling and its effects. They provided much thought for their own "green" initiatives.

This experience only served to highlight how life-changing a handmade gift can be, as it brightened the receiver and also managed to spark a conversation and change. Each of the soap dispensers was so much more than just a decorative detail: it represented a nudge toward sparking a greater consciousness of our planet. This was a very gratifying project, and I look forward to our class's creative ways of bringing back new life to things that are old and mundane.

"Looking Ahead"

Building on this success, I have been looking for other everyday items that I can similarly transform. My home is now filled with upcycled items that have these same stories of transformation and which still captivate my visitors and me with them. These dispensers are just the beginning. With increasing ease and agility, you will soon find the possibilities for your upcycling and creative works to be boundless. Project work that is not only good for the planet but also for the soul-fulfilling and practical use of your creativity.

Keep pushing, keep making, but remember: This isn't just about decoration; it's about the transformation of materials and, most importantly, of our mindset towards consumption and waste. So, let this project be another stride toward an even more sustainable and beautiful home. It is sure to be effective for you and good. Take this experience to heart, and be ready to have many more projects in the future!

Project 5: Reclaimed Wood Spice Rack

You've now established your position as one who succeeds in uncovering hidden potential in ordinary things, such as repurposed bottle soap dispensers. What's next on the frontier in your crafting odyssey? Let us delve deep into a project that combines working utility with rustic charm: a Reclaimed Wood Spice Rack. The project will not only add to the visual interest of your kitchen but also be in harmony with our philosophy of reuse and re-purpose.

Starting with the Basics

The first thing you need to do is find some reclaimed wood. Such treasure might come from defunct furniture, deserted pallets, or any source of sturdy wood that has been standing the test of time. Remarkably, very little exploratory effort can turn up surprisingly large finds, from neighbors to construction sites and local workshops, provided you approach with politeness.

Tools and Materials

Here's what you'll need to gather:

- Reclaimed wood planks
- Sandpaper or an electric sander
- Measuring tape
- Saw
- Screws and a drill
- Wood finish or paint
- Safety goggles and gloves

Building Your Spice Rack

- ***Measure and Cut***: Measure the wall space in your kitchen that you plan to put the spice rack in. Cut the wood planks into the measurements taken. A rough design sketch could help in judging the number of pieces that go into the rack.
- ***Sand and Prep***: The planks should be sanded down to lose all the rough surfaces and gain a glossy, splinter-free finish. Not for show purposes, though; this is done to avoid future splinters.
- ***Assemble***: lay out your pieces of wood and start fitting your rack together. You can keep it simple with just a few shelves or go a little more complex with some spice-jar slots. Attach your pieces of wood together with screws so that they are in place and square.

- ***Final touch***: Add a coat of wood finish or paint to enhance the beauty and at least protect the rack, especially when placed near areas that have a lot of cooking.

Customizing Your Creation

- ***Add Labels***: Add function flair to your shelves with labels, or use chalkboard paint and put it right on the shelves to create writable surfaces on the wood.
- ***Decorative Hooks***: You can attach small hooks under the shelves to hang your utensils or tea towels. This will serve the purpose and add some character.
- ***Light it Up***: Mount tiny LED lights underneath the shelves to create a light that illuminates the spices and affords your kitchen a warm feel.

Safety Alert! Always make safety your first priority when working with reclaimed wood and power tools. Wear safety gear and work in a well-ventilated environment while making sure your working area is free of clutter to eliminate potential hazards.

My Experience

Building my first reclaimed wood spice rack was an adventure if nothing else. I was making it for my sister, who was a really great cook but had a cluttered kitchen counter. It all started with one simple adventure: finding the wood. A friend was clearing the property, and underneath the brush, we found some weathered barn wood. Each of the planks had a character that could only have come from a past life.

That, in itself, added importance to the way we worked them into the kitchen. It was very fulfilling to create one that fit perfectly above the counter in her kitchen and to see how it changed her space. That project not only helped her get her spices in order but also lit the fire in me to continue to create functional art with salvaged materials.

"Looking Forward"

For this project, more than just construction is taking place—skill development, stimulation for creative solutions, and the promotion of sustainable practice. For each reclaimed wood piece diverted from the waste stream, steps are taken toward leading a more eco-conscious lifestyle. Your path goes beyond this project. The work that you will create past this very one will continue to infuse you with new confidence to take on the next bigger and better design. Whether working with much larger furniture or completely decorating your home, the skills, and principles learned while creating your spice rack will serve well and be a solid foundation. Keep on challenging yourself with new concepts. Each work is not just one more piece of work that adds to your home; it mirrors mindful living and your way toward sustainability. Enjoy the process, the sense of well-being, and the beauty it brings into your life on a daily basis. Give it a try and witness how these small projects can yield profound transformations in your home and mindset.

Project 6: Old Jeans Drawer Organizers

You are now a few successful reclaimed wood projects down and well on your way to becoming a serious craftsman, so here is another engrossing project: Old Jeans Drawer Organizers. You have the opportunity in this project to upcycle your old jeans that have been collecting dust in your closet into multipurpose, attractive, and functional drawer organizers. It's more about tidying up the space and restoring old fabrics by making things practical and beautiful.

Transforming Denim into Decor

Denim—it is so strong, and strong means ready for anything, like recycling. You'll find the high level of creativity that goes into repurposing old jeans when you work on this project. Turn your denim into a drawer organizer to stylishly declutter those drawers and bring new value into them, be it in the bedroom, kitchen, or home office.

Gathering Materials

For this project, you'll need:

- Old jeans
- Scissors
- Measuring tape
- Sewing machine or needle and thread
- Fabric glue (optional)

- Cardboard or any stiff material for structure

Steps to Create Your Denim Organizers

- ***Prepare the Jeans***: Start cutting up your jeans into panels using the big flat sections, generally representing the legs, to have several sizes according to your drawers' measurements.
- ***Measure and Cut Cardboard***: Measure the inside of your drawer, then cut the cardboard in the form of dividers to give shape to your organizers.
- ***Wrap and Sew***: Wrap and stitch the cardboard up with denim and stitch the edges to give a pocket, ensuring you get a firm and tidy finish. For those who do not like sewing, there is an alternative to using fabric glue, which serves as an excellent adhesive.
- ***Fit and Customize***: Place your newly designed denim organizers back into the drawers. Cut to size, and it should fit perfectly. Add labels or small compartments for your small items to enhance the level of customization.

Customizing Your Denim Organizers

- ***Pocket Potential***: Maximize pocket potential by utilizing the already existing pockets in jeans, then incorporating more segregated storage. These pockets are just perfect for keeping little things like jewelry or office supplies.
- ***Color Coordination***: They can be labeled by drawer or item type with the color of organizers using jeans of varied colors or tones.

- *Artistic Additions*: Personalize your organizers with buttons, patches, or embroidery.

Safety Alert! Be very careful to avoid passing scissors through the denim and the cardboard by providing a clear working space and always using sharp tools to prevent all forms of accidents. Watch the needle carefully as you sew; this is too strong a fabric like denim, which might make you miss a step.

Personal Experience

I remember that day like it was yesterday; on that day, I set out on a mission to convert a few old jeans into organizers for my drawers. That day meant serious spring cleaning, having literally come face to face with the excess of jeans that no longer fit the body. On a mission to upcycle them, my vision settled on the chaos that existed in my art supply drawers. The process started with selecting the most appealing denim jeans in terms of texture and color. I carefully cut the denim into varied shapes and sizes with the intention of fitting each piece into a designated drawer. As I worked, I observed that the fabric was so strong and perfect for holding some of the heavier products, like scissors and paint tubes.

Along with a friend, I spent an afternoon fashioning these blue jeans scraps into very personal organizers. We reinforced the back of the fabric with stiff cardboard so that we could sew the edges into pockets and compartments. It was a hands-on exercise in finding the value of existing resources. It was a real pleasure to be able to place the finished organizers in my drawers. I was so excited about the possibilities for each little section of denim—what it could contain—to really turn my ugly jumbled drawers into a beautiful storage paradise. It decluttered my space and got me inspired to get into upcycling and sewing as a creative way to deal with daily challenges.

"Looking Ahead"

This project, like the others, transcends the merely functional; it changes the way we think about trash and what it can be. It's a drawer organizer for your jeans, which in turn means one step further away from the landfill and possibly closer to zero-waste. Consider making more complex stuff with more experience or combining materials from multiple places into a single project for something a little more fancy. Maybe include the remnants of other upcycling projects or add some elements of reclaimed wood to the denim.

As you learn about the world of crafting, dare to deviate from the ordinary measures of creativity. Every project will fine-tune your skills and increase your determination to live sustainably. Look for ways to include diverse materials in your projects and experiment with new techniques. The more jobs you perform, the more you learn to enrich your ability to drive toward innovative and eco-sensitive solutions. Just go on creating and keep changing, as you see every new creation bring a little more order and beauty into your place and life.

CHAPTER 6

STYLISH ZERO-WASTE DECOR

So now, having conquered some of the easier projects, we embark on the more advanced journey into zero-waste home decor. Welcome to Chapter 6, where sustainability meets creativity in visually captivating ways. In this chapter, projects will be made in a way that recycles but also ups the aesthetic value of your living space. Be prepared to transform your textile scraps into beautiful woven wall hangings, your chipped ceramics into beautiful mosaics, and your leftover fabric into cool lampshades. All the projects are created with the maker's creative freedom, yet each project will raise the charm of your living space. Find detailed instructions, what you will need, and tips for each project, ensuring that everyone you create will be uniquely yours. They are more than just decoration pieces; they go beyond that, speaking of your decor and proving that sustainable living can actually be fashionable and elegant.

Project 7: Woven Wall Hangings from Textile Scraps

Now, onto Project 7: Woven Wall Hangings from Textile Scraps. With each project under your belt, your confidence and dexterity should be growing. So, with that in mind, I would like you to try this sweet, artistic project. Woven Wall Hangings are a creative and colorful way to use up those tiny leftover pieces of fabric that one cannot bear to throw away and marry sustainability with artistic expression in your home.

Turning Scraps into Art

"Taking scraps and turning them into art" means to make value out of what most people would consider trash: scrap bits of fabric left from the production of clothes, worn-out clothes, or bits and pieces of some other sewing project. In this project, we work on the process of producing woven wall hangings, or tapestries, by interlacing the different scraps of fabric into one integral piece.

With your decision to weave scrap textiles into a wall hanging, you are entering into more than just craft; you are entering an arena of mindful crafting. It's all mindful because one is very thoughtful about the resources' usage and the very act of creation, which could then take trash materials and turn them into useful art. Each strip of fabric and each piece of thread speaks their own story about where they came from, what they were before, and how it is finding a new life. The final result is a beautiful tapestry, a decoration in your home, and an expression of sustainability, always on display. What makes such wall hangings unique is that no two shall be exactly the same. They are an expression of the aesthetic choices of the crafter and specific materials. It's the transformation from a plain old scrap into an example of art that shows how creativity and eco-awareness can come together in the direction of something beautiful and beneficial to the environment.

Gathering Your Materials

For this project, you'll need:

- A wooden frame or an old picture frame—this will serve as your loom.
- A collection of textile scraps in various textures and colors.
- Scissors.
- A weaving needle or a large tapestry needle.
- Yarn or strong thread for the warp.

Crafting Your Woven Wall Hanging

- ***Prepare the Loom***: Working on a picture frame means taking out the glass and the back piece. Next, stretch your yarn taut right across the frame; these will be your warp threads, and you will weave your textiles right over the top of them.
- ***Sorting Your Textiles***: Sort your fabric scraps meticulously by color, texture, and length. You may wish to take into consideration the type of pattern or color gradation that you are after in your wall hanging.
- ***Start Weaving***: With your needle, begin weaving the fabric scraps under and over in the warp threads. In each row, push the fabric down hard, packing it tight together for a tight weave that will hold.

- ***Building the Design***: Weaving allows for the free use of many textures and colors. Whether you desire to create something with stripes in an orderly manner, chevrons for something very dynamic, or something abstract and free-flowing, every piece provides the next layer to your design.
- ***Securing the Edges***: As you weave toward the end of the frame, be sure to knot off your scraps at the ends securely. It's this fine detail that secures the weave in place and the integrity of the wall hanging together for years.

Personalizing Your Creation

- ***Add Embellishments***: Add beads, feathers, and other adornments to your weave for more flair and panache in your piece.
- ***Fringe Benefits***: Allow some threads to be released at the bottom of the wall hanging to create an amazing fringe at the base that will further build on the stylish look of your piece.
- ***Secure Hanging Hardware***: Secure a dowel rod or decorative branch to the top part of your wall hanging. This will assure you of a smooth, safe hanging process and that your creation is displayed in a way you can take pride in.

Safety Alert! Weaving is therapeutic; one can easily get lost in the process and forget about the tools. Be extremely cautious with the tools. Always keep your scissors safely stored when not in use, and handle the needle carefully when going through tight weaves.

Personal Experience

I love each one of them, and each one feels like a special journey. One of my favorite memories is creating my first woven wall hanging. What started out as a little experiment in the use of odd yarn leftovers and small pieces of fabric soon grew into an impressive artistic process. It would have been like painting with the fabric: picking up every piece, intertwining them, and seeing how colors and textures came together harmoniously. When I finally put it on my wall, instantly, the space changed and warmed with handmade charm. It was from one project only, from which it developed into one of my greatest hobbies, as so many wall hangings followed the first one. Each told a different story, a different mood, and an inspiration for change in my creativity. They also make touching gifts with a piece of my heart in each and a piece of expression.

"Looking Ahead"

Then, as you dive deeper into the world of weaving and creation, you notice that each wall hanging you make is not just a decorative part of your living room but also has a sense of meaning within the materials you are using. This is no ordinary craft; it is a living testimony of deep connections with the environment that asserts sustainability in living through creative means. The challenge and joy in this project come from understanding that skills developed unlock new realms of artistic exploration and home adornment. Remember, as you create each piece, you are proving to yourself and the world that there is a possibility of a constructive transformation through imagination and a commitment to repurpose materials that are otherwise labeled waste. Both your home and life are enriched with every thread and scrap.

Project 8: Mosaic Art from Broken Ceramics

Now that you've mastered wall hangings using scraps of textiles, it is high time to proceed with mosaic art using broken ceramics. Creatively, you will learn how to look at broken objects not just as the end of something but rather as the beginning of creating something beautiful.

Creating Beauty from Brokenness

Mosaic creates beauty out of imperfection: it breathes new life into remains of what was once whole, be it beloved but fractured dishes, chipped tiles, or eclectic finds from thrift stores. The pursuit of creativity breathes a second, dynamic life into materials that would otherwise decay and be forgotten. In a finished mosaic, you move beyond simple recycling; it is a personal statement, creating something as unique and expressive as a signature intended to enhance your house's appeal.

My initiation into the world of mosaic art was completely accidental and occurred while visiting a local craft market. I had the most experienced hands, and in the middle of them all, there was ***a boy who was probably not over ten years old***. With precision and care, like an experienced craftsman, he was making mosaic floral compositions from broken ceramics. His tiny hands joined the broken shards into small blooming flowers with fine petals and tiny emerald leaves. What this budding artist saw and did that others did not was the potential to discard, transforming broken fragments into something so beautiful and alive. He found that pure joy, the well of unlimited creativity that only art can unleash into the open. What touched me most was the view he cast upon the broken pieces, not as desolate but as bearing some latent beauty, and it went past the aesthetic perception of the art. This was the most touching: art is not for pleasure; indeed, it is a mighty tool for reshaping the way we view our reality. The inventiveness in his inspired me, and I came back to my own work with greater energy and determination, resolved to infuse my mosaics with the same kind of transformational magic that had so captivated me.

Collecting Your Materials

For this project, you will need:

- Broken pieces of ceramics
- Safety goggles and gloves to protect yourself from sharp edges
- A sturdy base for your mosaic (this could be a tabletop, a picture frame backing, or a simple wooden board)
- Tile adhesive
- Grout
- A putty knife or a similar spreading tool
- A sponge and a bucket of water for cleaning

Constructing Your Mosaic

- ***Prepare the Base***: Select and clear away dirt and moisture from the base, as it will establish the foundation on which the ceramic pieces will lay.
- ***Design Your Artwork***: Arrange the ceramic pieces on the base before sticking them to form a pattern. Whether geometric or floral, abstract or any other design, take your time to finalize the layout.
- ***Removing the Pieces***: After completing the arrangement, you should start fixing every piece of ceramic by using the tile adhesive. In this process, you need to wear gloves and be cautious since the pieces should be close-fitting to one another.
- ***Grouting***: After the adhesive is dry (usually overnight), the piece should be grouted by applying grout over the piece evenly to fill the gaps between the ceramic fragments. This will provide your artwork with more stability and, at the same time, add a visual touch.
- ***Finishing Touches***: Use a moist sponge to clean up the grout, leaving your ceramic pieces restored with nothing to take away from them.

Customizing Your Mosaic Piece

Colorful Grout Choices: Try bright grout colors to add color and impact your mosaic work instead of the usual plain white or gray grout.

Incorporate Quotes or Shapes: You might also decide to lay out your ceramic pieces so that they spell a word or are symbolic of something that's important to you.

Add Other Elements: To add an extra touch of texture and depth, incorporate such design elements as glass beads, old jewelry pieces, or metal pieces in your mosaic design.

Safety Alert! Working with damaged ceramics always carries the risk of cuts from the sharp edges. Always wear safety goggles and protective gloves when cutting and handling the pieces. Keep your working area clean to eliminate potential accidents.

Personal Experience

My very first mosaic project was an interesting adventure. It all started many years ago when a special ceramic bowl, a gift from a friend, was accidentally dropped and broken into pieces. Seeing a new project the pieces of that broken bowl went into a new project that summer: a small tabletop to grace my living room with a focal point centerpiece of color. The project was not just about crafting but a meaningful reminder of impermanence and renewal. His family and friends, who filed past the table at the end of it all, saw beauty in the concept of sustainability and creative reuse of available material. It was really fulfilling to realize that through such a project, I was able to say that beauty is most certainly revealed in the least expected forms.

"Looking Ahead"

Every mosaic is an impression of your walk through this world of sustainable artistry. With every developed skill, there is another level to open one's creativity and personal expression. It would be well to stress again that this is not merely decorative; it is about inscribing the world with your singular soul. It is about how even fragments can be reinvented with a touch of innovation. As you experiment further and learn more about the craft of mosaic, each piece becomes so much more than a decoration; it becomes an extension of you as an artist. Each pattern you bring to life stretches the boundaries of what can be created from so much cast-off material. Each work of art goes beyond decoration to embody a true testament to your creativity and conviction for the Earth. Keep on exploring new ways and new sources of inspiration. May your creations inspire not only your creativity but others as well. As you keep growing in your craft, you will get to notice how your works keep growing from just materials to amazing stories of transformation and new beginnings. Embrace this craft wholeheartedly and observe how it reshapes materials and, in the process, reshapes your concept of art and sustainability.

Project 9: Lampshades from Upcycled Fabric

You learned how broken ceramic tiles are turned into mosaics and quite likely gained some measure of confidence, all by completing a small project. So, you are just about ready to move on to another project that will bring a bit more of a touch of sustainability into your home. Making cool lampshades that light up your room and make the very presence of them light a spotlight on your own ability to recycle. That's right. Shed some light on your living spaces and your commitment to creative recycling with "Upcycled Fabric Lampshades."

Breathing New Life into Old Fabric

In every household are residues of old curtains, pieces of worn-out clothes, or pieces of your work that you can't throw away, but you don't know what to use them for. These are all given new life in the making of beautiful lampshades. It's one very fitting case in point to show the transformation power of creativity in that almost anything can be remodeled into something new and useful.

Gathering Your Tools and Materials

To start, you'll need:

- Old fabric pieces large enough to cover your lampshade frames
- Lampshade frames (you can repurpose old ones or buy basic wireframes)
- Fabric glue or a hot glue gun
- Scissors
- Optional: Decorative elements such as ribbons, lace, or beads

Creating Your Upcycled Lampshades

- ***Preparing the Fabric***: Measure and cut the fabric according to your lampshade frame, making sure that you leave extra fabric on all sides to finish it neatly.
- ***Attaching the Fabric***: Spread the fabric glue all over the lampshade frame and lay your fabric on the frame, straightening wrinkles or bubbles.
- ***Edge the Lampshade***: Fold the remaining fabric on the edge over it and stick it down strong to secure the edges of the lampshade and make it look professional and really polished.
- ***Personalizing Your Design***: If you are creative, you can add in decorative trims by way of lace or ribbon on the top and bottom edges of the lampshade, together with beads or other decorative enhancements for more aesthetics.

Safety Alert! Always take care of the use of fabric glue and the hot glue gun. Work only in a well-ventilated room, be sure to wear gloves to protect from burns, and keep the working area clean to avoid any accidents.

Personal Experience

Being able to make a lampshade out of repurposed fabric is an experience I shall never forget; it was simply memorable. I used some old-style curtains that had once hung in my grandmother's window. They are softly faded and have a delicate floral pattern, very much like hers in her garden. Making a lampshade from them, I felt like I was preserving something more than just a piece of family history; it became something that doubled up as a great conversation piece and was much loved by all who saw it. Each time I put the light on, I feel that I bring a little piece of her warmth back to my home.

"Looking Ahead"

As you continue with the search for making lampshades out of upcycled cloth, every new creation can be much more than simply an addition to the beauty of your living space; it can reflect who you are. Every new lampshade you create pushes the envelope farther back on what is possible with products destined for the refuse pile. Such projects will be enjoyed every inch of the way, and they display your commitment to sustainability.

Experiment with different fabrics, textures, and colors—add beads and embroidery, or whichever type of personal embellishment—where each personal shade will speak for itself. Share your final creations with your friends and family to inspire some conversations about sustainable living. It is just the next step to doing better and exploring new possibilities in design. You may move on to lighting or home décor totally. The possibilities are just endless, and every creation is a step forward on your creative journey.

Go at everything with enthusiasm and curiosity. Every scrap of fabric upcycled or the room you have brightened contributes to making a difference in this world. So, let's move forward, explore options, and keep innovating one gorgeous lampshade at a time. Keep shining that little light of yours; you truly make a difference in more ways than one!

CHAPTER 7

SEASONAL AND GIFT PROJECTS

Chapter 7 invites you to listen to the heart of each season while at the same time supporting the spirit of giving through sustainable crafting. In this section, we start a journey of turning some common household waste into festive arrays of gift creations, decorations, and seasonal wreaths. This, in turn, will fill your abode with holiday cheer and give you a glimpse of our no-waste living path.

Project 10: Festive Décorations from Household Waste

Using household waste, we have demonstrated how to make festive decorations in Project 10 and bring in the holiday mood by using your crafting skills.

Project 10.1: Bottle cap décor

These cute little decorations are a great way to recycle your used bottle tops. All they need is some paint and a pinch of creativity to make a great decoration. Glue on some glitter or hang them with a ribbon. This funny project will involve all the family members and add a lot of personality, with an ecological touch, to your decorations.

Each ornament is a mini canvas to be expressive of your very own personal style, or it can be reminiscent of holiday sentiments—thus, your tree will be absolutely beautiful and individual. To start your festive journey with bottle cap ornaments, arrange all your materials in advance for an easy craft experience.

Materials Needed:

- Bottle caps (collected from used beverages)
- Non-toxic paint (in various colors)
- Paintbrushes
- Glitter or glitter glue
- Ribbons or string for hanging
- Hot glue gun (optional for attaching ribbons)
- Small holiday-themed decorations like tiny bells or holly (optional)

Step-by-Step Instructions

- ***Bottle Caps***: Prepare the bottle caps very well by washing and drying them. In case of any sharp edges, use a metal file to rub them off so that no incident occurs while manipulating them.
- ***Paint the Lids***: Paint all your bottle caps with your favorite base paint. You may want to go with the usual festive shades of red, green, and gold, or go ahead and mix up a bunch to match your room's palette. Wait for the paint to dry completely before proceeding to the next step.
- ***Add Designs***: Now that the basecoat is dry, let your imagination go wild. Paint festive symbols, like stars,

Christmas trees, or snowflakes on the caps. If you are looking for something a little bit more basic, you can apply a second coat in a contrasting color and then design using the end of a brush.

- ***Sprinkle Some Glitter***: If you happen to be using paint while it's still wet, sprinkle some glitter on the caps. If you are using glitter glue, just wait until the paint has dried and then apply it.
- ***Attach the Hangers***: Cut the ribbon or string into 6-inch pieces. Use a hot glue gun to glue one end of the ribbon inside each of the bottle caps. Optionally, you could punch a tiny hole near the edge of the cap and string the ribbon through the hole, tying a little knot.
- ***Final Touches***: Finally, you may wish to add some further embellishments, such as tiny bells, little pieces of holly, or whatever you wish – to the ribbon or tinsel or to the caps directly with a hot glue gun for an extra festive flourish.

Customization Tips

- ***Personal Touch***: You can also include initials or important dates for every other cap; this will make the ornaments more special as gifts or keepsakes. The personalization of these ornaments gives them a warm touch and definitely an assurance of uniqueness for every piece.
- ***Theme Variations***: Be creative with colors and decorations that would fit themes of various holidays like Hanukkah, New Year's bashes, and any other festive moments. Your color

scheme and theme-based ornaments add another level of charm and cohesion to your holiday decor.

- ***Group Craft Project***: Make creating bottle cap ornaments a fun and memorable group activity by involving the people around you. Come up with your ideas around the craft table and bring your holiday decorations to life as you enjoy the sense of community this will bring. Bring more to share, more to enjoy—bring more togetherness.
- ***Eco-Friendly Twist***: Decorate your hat with small seeds or leaves for glitter, and it will contribute to a more rustic and organic look than the usual glitter. In addition, it reduces the carbon footprint because you won't use all that extra energy for sourcing and shipping traditional glitter. It is a great way to show that you are an environmentally conscious person making beautiful holiday decorations.

Project 10.2: Tin Can Lanterns

Turning normal tin cans into delightful lanterns is a creative process that adds some soft ambient light around you and sets the mood indoors and outdoors at nighttime. They make great lights-and-shadows designs in any setting, adding a touch of magic. Tin can lanterns are good at combining functionality with charm, whether in festive arrangements or as regular decor. Make sure to have your materials ready before you start your project, and prepare your working area accordingly.

Materials Needed:

- Empty tin cans (cleaned and labels removed)
- Hammer and large nail or a drill
- Spray paint or regular paint
- Tea lights or small LED candles
- Protective gloves
- Towel or soft surface to work on

Step-by-Step Instructions

- ***Prepare the Can***: Fill the cans with water, then freeze them solid overnight. This way, the cans will be stabilized, and you will need not worry about getting any dents while making holes.
- ***Punching Hole***: When water is frozen solid, take the hammer and nail or drill and punch holes into the can in any sort of design you'd like. Doing this over a soft surface is best to help avoid slipping. Make anything from simple stars and moons to more complex geometric designs.
- ***Spray Paint***: After all of the ice has melted and the can has dried thoroughly, spray paint with your favorite color. Use metallic colors, like silver, gold, or copper, for a touch of class or bright colors if you're in a festive mood and want it to be fun.
- ***Insert the light source***: When the paint is fully dry, insert a tea light or a small LED candle into the can. For a real candle and to have it safe, just make a small opening at the top to get rid of the excess heat.

- ***Hanging or Placing Your Lantern***: Hang your lanterns with wire or place them along a pathway, table, or windowsill for both lighting and decor, with their beautiful patterns of light and shadow.

Customization Tips

- ***Varied Design***: Experiment with different hole patterns and designs to discover how light plays with each variation. Themed designs, such as snowflakes for a wintertime holiday feel or hearts for Valentine's Day, all create seasonal charm within your lanterns.
- ***Add Handles***: Add to the practicality of your lanterns with wire handles that will make it easy for you to hang them in any chosen spot. Be it a tree or hooks or on the porch—hang them in all possible ways to get the best ambiance for your place.
- ***Grouped Displays***: Uplift your game in decor by clustering together an assortment of lanterns of different heights and styles. When clustered, you have quite an interesting, dynamic display that captures your eye and adds depth to your surroundings.

Safety Alert! Pay attention to the safety of your space, especially if you're using real candles. Watch them when they're burning to prevent a fire hazard as much as possible. Other choices are the use of safe, reusable LED candles that throw off the same kind of magical light.

Project 10.3: Jar Snow Globes

This mason jar snow globe doesn't just encase magical winter spirit in a tiny glass jar; it's an enchanting decoration or kind of gift. Old glass jars turned into an appealing miniature scene filled with water, which sends them over the top. It's a magnificent way to bring some more magic into your decoration for a wonderful holiday. Then, gather everything you may need for this creative journey and be sure that your workplace is clean and organized.

Materials Needed:

- Glass jars with tight-sealing lids
- Distilled water
- Glycerin (to thicken the water and slow the glitter fall)
- Glitter or fake snow
- Waterproof glue (like epoxy or silicone sealant)
- Small waterproof figurines or holiday decorations
- Optional: small pebbles or sand (for additional weight and scenery)

Step-by-Step Instructions

Creating your own jar snow globes is so much fun, as you are going to be able to make a small magical world just inside the glass jar with winter scenes. You can follow the steps below to create yours.

- ***Prepare the Jar***: Start by making sure the glass jars are clean; they should also be fully dry. While you can use jars of any size, the ones with wide mouths make it easy to assemble the scenes.

- *Attach the Figurines*: Attach whatever holiday decorations or figurines you have chosen to the inside of the jar lid with the waterproof glue. Think along the lines of miniature trees, animals, or other holiday personages. Let set and dry thoroughly.
- *Mix the Snow Solution*: Fill the jar almost to the top with distilled water. Take a teaspoon of glycerin and add it to water; this will make the glitter float and fall slowly. Sprinkle some good glitter or fake snow into the water to give a snowing effect.
- *Assemble the Globe*: Once the figurines are well-stuck and the glue is dry, carefully screw the jar's lid back on, ensuring it is tight so there are no leaks.
- *Seal the Lid*: With waterproof adhesive, run a bead around the opening of the jar where the lid will screw down on the jar. Let the glue dry before moving on.
- *Shake and Enjoy*: Shake your completed snow globe so the snow or glitter swirls all around the inside of your merry little scene. Display proudly and enjoy the magic atmosphere brought to your space.

Customization Tips

Take your jar snow globes a step above the rest with these personalization ideas to make stunning, one-of-a-kind scenes:

- ***Scenic Bases***: Elevate your snow globe scenes with a base layer of small pebbles, colored sand, or moss. These additions provide depth and texture to your miniature world, making it even more appealing.
- ***Themed Snow Globes***: You can theme your snow globes, both inside and outside, to suit various occasions. Be it a snowy forest, a winter wonderland, or a beach scene for a whimsical twist, let your imagination run with wild ideas to create engaging scenes that are full of joy and wonder.
- ***Exterior Decor***: Dress up your snow globes made from jars from the outside. A few ideas: Use paint, ribbon, or adhesive jewels to dress up the outside of the jar, just like you might frame a picture, adding to the festiveness and specialness of the scene inside. Tying elements together not only enhances the already-stated concept but also adds to the visual presentation of the globe.
- ***Light it Up***: Add some light to those snow globes. Just pop a little battery tea light under the jar. The light is so soft and will reflect from under, giving your set just the right feel. It will be charming and magical for all.

Project 10.4 CD Mosaic Frames

Turn your old, scratched CDs into mosaic frames that will catch the eyes of many. Ideal for any photo or other artwork, with just a little bit of sparkle and a touch of creativity for all that the design of your house needs. This project not only helps give new life to CDs that might otherwise be trashed but also allows for artistic expression without increased waste. So gather everything you are going to need and set up your workspace for a little crafty fun and adventure.

Materials Needed:

- Old CDs
- A photo frame (any size will do, but larger frames may require more CDs)
- Scissors or a utility knife
- Strong glue or a hot glue gun
- Grout (optional, depending on your aesthetic preference)
- Cloth and a little soapy water (for cleaning)

Step-by-Step Instructions

Just follow these simple step-by-step instructions to make your incredible CD mosaic picture frames:

- ***Prepare the CDs***: Carefully cut the CDs into various shapes and sizes using scissors or a utility knife. To make it easier to cut, you might want to soak the CDs in some hot water for a few minutes before cutting them.
- ***Design Your Mosaic***: Lay out your CD pieces on the frame first before you glue them down to experiment with some designs and patterns. Use reflective sides up for maximum sparkle.
- ***Glue the Pieces***: Now, start to glue the CD pieces one by one around the frame with a good strong glue or, better yet, with hot glue, leaving it well adapted so that each of the pieces is tightly held in place.

- ***Grouting (optional)***: Grout in between the CD pieces, which gives a more classic mosaic look once the adhesive has dried. Spread the grout with a very even hand and remove the excess with a damp cloth. Follow the instructions on the grouting pack for setting time.
- ***Clean and Finish***: After the grout has dried and the glue has set, use a cloth dipped in warm, soapy water to wipe off the residue glue or grout haze from the CD pieces.

Customization Tips

These are some pointers on how to go about personalizing your mosaic frames made with CD:

- ***Color Play***: Use CDs that differ in reflective colors in order to get a vibrant effect. The interplay of light will result in unique shows of color at different angles from the CDs.
- ***Frame Size and Shape***: Play around with different sizes and shapes of frames to add more to your mosaic. For instance, a round frame would just go perfectly as it showcases the mosaic effect in a very pretty way.
- ***Additional Decorations***: Further spruce up your frame by including other decorative items between the pieces of CD, such as beads or small mirrors. This will give your mosaic art some depth and mystery.
- ***Usage Variations***: The technique has lots of varied uses apart from making photo frames. Use it to decorate mirror borders or to make small table tops or decorative wall hangings.

Project 11: Handcrafted Eco-Friendly Gift Ideas

This section is filled with great ideas for personalized, special gifts whose thoughtfulness is reflected in them, with adherence to the basics of eco-friendly principles. Each—from beeswax candles to herbal sachets—offers the opportunity to give a gift that keeps on giving, both to your recipient and to the environment.

Project 11.1 Homemade Beeswax Candles

Indulge in the warm, cozy art of candle making by creating your very own beeswax candles. These homemade delights bring not just warmth but also the charm of nature, with absolutely no chemicals, unlike their commercially available counterparts. Infused with essential oils, they make any space filled with calming fragrances, therefore uplifting the quality of the atmosphere as well as the air. First, gather all the materials you need and prepare your space for the most amazing and satisfying adventure in your crafting career.

Materials Needed:

- Beeswax (pellets or blocks)
- Candle wicks
- Double boiler or a similar setup for melting wax
- Essential oils (optional for fragrance)
- Natural dyes (optional for color)

- Molds or containers for the candles (can be old jars, teacups, etc.)
- Thermometer (to monitor wax temperature)
- Stirring stick

Step-by-Step Instructions

- ***Preparing Your Molds***: Start by placing the wicks inside the containers or molds you are using. An easy way to do this is by placing a pencil or stick across the top of the mold so that the wick is tied around it, sitting in the center of the container.
- ***Melting the Wax***: If you are to put the beeswax in a double boiler to carry out a low-heating process, you can break chunks of beeswax blocks into smaller pieces to help in the melting process.
- ***Temperature Monitoring***: The monitoring of wax temperature should be done using a thermometer. Ideally, beeswax should melt at around 145°F (63°C) so that it will burn properly and efficiently without overburning.
- ***Adding Color and Scent***: Once the wax is fully melted, throw in the natural dyes and essential oils for a pleasant smell and color. Mix everything well until the color and aroma are properly distributed into the wax.
- ***Pour Melted Wax***: Into the Prepared Molds: Carefully pour the wax into the prepared molds, making sure that the wick remains centered as you pour the wax.
- ***Allowing to Set***: Allow sufficient time for the candles to cool and harden completely, requiring many hours in general,

depending on the size of the candle and the environmental conditions.

- *Trim the Wick*: Once the wax is fully set, trim the wick to 1/4 inch over the top of the wax.

Customization Tips

- *Blended Aroma*: Different essential oils can be used together in order to get the desired scent. Examples might include using lavender and chamomile in combination to result in a calming blended aroma of citrus combined with mint for something more invigorating.
- *Decorative Additions*: Make it more aesthetically appealing by simply tossing some herbs, spices, or dried flowers at the bottom of the mold before pouring the wax in. This will give a sweet botanical effect to the candles.
- *Personal* **Touch**: Go for molds or containers of the liking or interest of the individual so that the candle becomes a personalized gift specific to his style.

Project 11.2 Seed Paper Greeting Cards

Celebrate life's moments with handmade greeting cards that each hold a very special surprise. With wildflower, herb, or vegetable seeds in the fiber, your message in a seed paper greeting card can be read and then planted to become flourishing plants. The environmentally friendly cards take your sentiments to growing reminders of care.

Gather all the necessary materials and prepare a work area.

Materials Needed:

- Recycled paper (could be from newspapers, magazines, or old stationery)
- Seeds (choose wildflower, herb, or vegetable seeds that are small and flat)
- Blender or food processor
- Large basin or tub
- Warm water
- Screen or mesh (for the papermaking frame)
- Sponge
- Rolling pin or large can
- Iron (optional)
- Decorative stamps or markers (for decorating)
- Natural dyes (optional for coloring the paper)

Step-by-Step Instructions

- ***Prepare the Paper Pulp***: Tear the recycled papers into bits, then soak them in warm water for several hours so that they soften. When they are softened, pour them into a blender, add some warm water, and finally blend until you have a smooth pulp.
- ***Mix in the Seeds***: Gently combine seeds of your choice with pulp base so that they become well distributed in the mix. The mixing should be light in order not to break the seeds.
- ***Form the Paper***: Pour the pulp mixture into a basin of water. Then, put the paper-making screen into the basin and carefully

scoop the pulp onto the screen. Carefully move the mass back and forth on the screen for uniform distribution.

- ***Dry the Paper***: Lift the screen gently from the water and let any extra water drip off. Again, press the pulp down using a sponge to squeeze out the excess water further. After this, the screen is lifted from the paper, and the paper is transferred to a cloth or another nonstick surface. You can flatten and smoothen the paper with a rolling pin. The paper must be dried in the air or by using an iron to speed the process up.
- ***Cut and Decorate***: Once the paper is completely dry, you may cut the paper to your size for your greeting card. Be creative; you can decorate your cards with stamps, markers, or natural dyes. Do this with caution so as not to destroy the seeds inside the paper.

Customization Tips

- ***Seed Selection***: Customize the seeds selected to be placed within the card based on the interests of the person receiving the card. For example, herbs can be selected for a cooking lover, wildflowers for a nature lover, or vegetables for a gardener.
- ***Personal Messages***: Customize them with some notes written or some of your sketches. Make use of some environmentally friendly inks to keep the content of the card in line with the principles of eco-friendliness.

- ***Decorative Edges***: Add a little more appeal to cards by trimming them with fancy-edged scissors. Give them fancy-cut borders, just for a bit of delight and class in the design.
- ***Packaging***: Gift the cards in upcycled envelopes to subtly bring out the eco-friendly status of your gift. You can even include the steps for planting the seed paper inside each envelope, nudging the recipients to enjoy the complete card.

Project 12.3 Herbal Potpourri Sachets

You can enjoy one of those old-time favorite pastimes and create fragrant sachets filled with dried herbs and flowers that let out all their natural and relaxing fragrances. Herbal potpourri sachets emit soft, green smells that can be placed in drawers, closets, or cars. These herbal potpourri sachets make excellent projects in which to use up those garden herbs and flowers, creating wonderful and useful gifts for friends and family. To get started on the project, organize your materials and set up your workspace so everything is ready:

Materials Needed:

- Dried herbs and flowers (like lavender, rose petals, mint, and chamomile)
- Essential oils (optional for enhancing the fragrance)
- Small cloth bags or fabric scraps and ribbon (if making your own bags)
- Scissors
- Spoon or funnel (for filling the sachets)
- Bowl (for mixing the herbs and flowers)

Step-by-Step Instructions

- ***Prepare Herbs and Flowers***: You have to start with the dehydrated herbs and flowers you are using. When dry, lightly crush them to a smaller size, but don't go as far as to make them into a powder; you want to see some texture and look to them.
- ***Enhance the Scent***: To this herb and flower mixture, add a small amount of essential oil to boost the fragrance and contribute to the treatment properties of the sachets. Thoroughly mix the ingredients, but gently enough to avoid spilling oil everywhere.
- ***Fill the Sachets***: Open the premade cloth bags and use a spoon or funnel to fill them with your herbal mixture. Or make them from scratch: cut small squares or circles from fabric scraps. Put a good tablespoon of the herbal mixture in the center of each piece of fabric. Bring up the edges, tying them securely with ribbon.
- ***Seal and Finish***: Ensure that the bags are well-tied to avoid the spilling of contents. Slightly shake each sachet to allow it to pour its fragrant scent.

Customization Tips

- ***Personalized Fabrics***: Choose a color and pattern of fabric that the recipient loves or that would best suit the theme of the sachets. Think about more discrete patterns for lingerie drawers and brighter colors for sachets for cars.

- ***Herbal Blends***: The mixes of herbs can be tailored to the pallet or to the intention of use of the user. One that can be made up for relaxation would include lavender and chamomile, while one for energizing would be peppermint and citrus peel.
- ***Decorative Touches***: Personalize your sachets with small charms, lace, or other little decorated, possibly embroidered embellishments.
- ***Gift Presentation***: Pack a number of sachets into a gift box or basket, nicely decorated, and describe somewhat all the blends and benefits so that the recipient of this gift will appreciate it more.

Project 12: Seasonal Wreaths from Natural Materials

Welcome to our exquisite wreaths guide, combining all the natural beauty of the seasons: each of the projects is designed to bring out the unique appeal and colors of the seasons in evergreen branches, lively wildflowers, or autumn leaves to your home.

Project 12.1 Autumn Leaf Wreath

Fall brings bright colors. Dive into the colors of autumn with this beautiful wreath made out of the brightest and most colorful leaves of the season. It's an easy, fast, and attractive project that arrests the ephemeral beauty of fall, bringing its warmth with it onto your doorstep or walls, making it an appealing part of your seasonal decorations.

Have everything ready for this project and prepare your workspace so it can host a little bit of nature indoors.

Materials Needed:

- A variety of colorful autumn leaves (the more colors and shapes, the better)
- A wreath base (this can be a wire frame, grapevine, or even a foam circle)
- Floral wire or hot glue gun
- Clear sealant spray (to help preserve the leaves and their vibrant colors)
- Ribbon or twine for hanging

Step-by-Step Instructions

- ***Leave Collection and Preparation***: Take a walk in the park and collect leaves on the ground in all colors and shapes. Collect mainly whole leaves without damage. Make them lie flat and spray both sides with a clear sealant spray, which will protect their color and keep them from drying up too soon. Let them dry completely.
- ***Add the Leaves***: Go ahead and place all your leaves onto the frame without gluing them. Try a few different designs until you are happy with one. You will want to place them in a

shingled pattern, one on top of the other, to get a really thick and full look.

- ***Attach Leaves***: After you are happy with the way the leaves are arranged, you will have to begin attaching them to the base. This can be done traditionally with floral wire, or if you're in a hurry and don't plan on disassembling the headpiece, just use a hot glue gun—the glue will strengthen the attachment and speed up the process. When using wire, always work from the outer edge so that each subsequent layer will overlap the previous one a little, thus hiding the base and all the attachment points.
- ***Final Touches***: Once all the leaves are put in position and well fixed, other decorative accessories can further detail the wreath using such things as small pine cones, acorns, or clusters of berries. Attach a ribbon or twine at the back.

Customization Tips

- ***Color Variations***: Use leaves from many species of trees. Try to get a wide variety of colors and textures. Some leaves turn color sooner, so you'll want to keep adding fresh ones to keep the design as current as the season.
- ***Add Lights***: String in a series of battery-operated fairy lights to set a magical feel.
- ***Indoor/Outdoor Use***: If looking to utilize the wreath outside, put it in an area that is a bit more protected so the weather does not get to it. Inside use will generate a great centerpiece for a dining room table with a fall theme.

Project 12.2 Evergreen and Pinecone Wreath

This classically wintery wreath mixes the bright, rich greens of evergreen branches with the rustic appeal of pinecones for a result that's at home in holiday and winter decorating. It's really alive with a little piece of peaceful winter woodland, radiating a natural warmth and festive ambiance.

Prepare your work area and needed supplies in advance of any creation to make the process smooth and without any hitches.

Materials Needed:

- Evergreen branches (such as pine, fir, or spruce)
- Pinecones of various sizes
- Floral wire
- Wreath base (wire or grapevine bases work best for support)
- Gardening shears or scissors
- Optional: ribbon, spray snow, or artificial berries for additional decoration

Step-by-Step Instructions

- ***Prepare the Base***: With grapevine wreaths, for extra support in areas that seem to be loose, add in additional pieces of floral wire to help hold the base together. For bases made out of wire, bulk them up by wrapping them in floral tape.
- ***Add Evergreen Branches***: Cut evergreen branches to a workable size—say, from 6 to 10 inches—and then bind them

with floral wire onto the wreath base, layering one over the other so as to cover the entire base in a very lush manner.

- ***Add Pinecones***: String the pinecones evenly through the wreath with floral wire, then wrap the wire around the base of the cone to secure it to the form for balance.
- ***Decorative Accents***: Add a ribbon bow, spray of snow for a frosty effect, or artificial berries for color. Attach these with a floral wire or by hot gluing in place on the wreath.
- ***Finishing Touches***: Make sure that everything is secured in place and well covered at the base. Trim off unnecessary branches and any other final touches to the decorations that need doing.

Customization Tips

- ***Theme Options***: Change out the accessories on your wreath to some wintry themes. For a more elegant appearance, add some silver or gold spray-painted pine cones with some sparkly embellishments.
- ***Fragrance***: To create a beautiful seasonal smell, attach natural scents of pine or cedarwood to cones or branches.
- ***Lighting***: You can use LED fairy lights inside the wreath; they give off a warm, welcoming glow for a great nighttime ambiance.

Project 12.3 Wildflower and Herb Wreath

Greet the explosion of summer and spring hues with this lively wreath, handcrafted from a medley of wildflowers and fragrant herbs.

Splashes of color and texture will be added to your décor, but it will also fill your space with the delightful scents of the garden, hence adding to the ambiance and beauty from the outdoors that only nature can hold.

Get your work area set up and gather all your supplies ready to make this beautiful, nature-inspired wreath.

Materials Needed:

- A variety of fresh or dried wildflowers and herbs (such as lavender, rosemary, chamomile, and mint)
- Grapevine wreath base or wireframe
- Floral wire
- Gardening shears
- Optional: ribbon or burlap for hanging

Step-by-Step Instructions

- ***Prepare Your Materials***: Select newly picked wildflowers and herbs in their freshest condition, preferably early in the morning when their fragrance is at its peak. Dried materials should be pliable and soft. They might need to be sprayed very lightly with water to avoid breakage.
- ***Attach Your Greens***: Begin creating a base by layering some of the larger herbs and foliage on the base of your wreath form. Fasten them in place with some floral wire, which can be wrapped around the stems and the base to hold them in place tightly.

- ***Place Wildflowers***: Now that the foundation is in place, randomly put wildflowers between the gaps of herbs, giving an infusion of colors and scents. Attach each stem with floral wire to secure and maintain the shape of the wreath.
- ***Fill and Secure***: Fill in any gaps with more greenery or foliage, and secure loose ends by using more of your floral wire. You want this to look full and natural; add volume by continually making adjustments to keep it symmetrical.
- ***Finishing Touches***: Stand back and look at your wreath as a whole. Balance the design with any needed changes, and then trim off any showing stems, which helps give a clean finish.

Customization Tips

- ***Seasonal-Adaptable***: Make your wreath seasonal by choosing blossoms and herbs that bloom at any time of year. For instance, sunflowers and daisies should be used during summer, or tulips and hyacinths should be used during spring.
- ***Decorative Additions***: A nice addition with a bow of an attractive decoration or a bit of rustic ribbon makes up your wreath.
- ***Fragrance Combinations***: Experiment with different blends of herbs for changing smells. Lavender and mint give an invigorating smell; rosemary and thyme have a hearty aroma.
- ***Preservation***: Spray floral preservatives on your wreath to keep it alive and fresh, especially when using fresh materials.

Now that we have come to the end of these projects, it is time to realize it is more than just crafting; it's an initiative in the line of sustainable and creative living. We encourage you not just to adopt these ideas but to think outside of the box and bring your own creative ideas into your home decor. By so doing, you will be recycling materials, reducing clutter, and helping to make the planet a better place. Farther than providing a habitat improvement, each small project nurtures your zero-waste mentality toward a rewarding and sustainable lifestyle in the long run. Take on the projects with glee and let your creative mind lead the way to a greener, cleaner world.

CHAPTER 8

ZERO-WASTE LIVING BEYOND DÉCOR

We will learn how to expand zero-waste practices beyond our homes and how to integrate them into our daily lives when out shopping or on a social night. Together, we help each other build a strong community network and encourage and support each other to sustain these for the long run. We empower one another by sharing how to reduce waste in our workplaces, how to organize eco-friendly events, and power such events in our neighborhoods. Are you ready to continue this journey toward a zero-waste life in every decision that betters our planet and creates a brighter future? Let's embark on this journey together!

Extending Zero-Waste Practices

With twelve projects behind us, the skill base in creating sustainable home décor is now solid; we have learned a great deal and have an increased sense of respect for materials and what they can become. It is an opportune moment to really weave these lessons into the very fabric of our lives.

Just imagine: you're sitting in a beautiful, waste-free, upcycled sanctuary with all kinds of knickknacks around your shelves that are recycled or repurposed and art on your walls that is repurposed. But wait, let's not stop there. Look outside your house one step further. Go all the way to what defines your lifestyle—what you eat, what you wear, the garbage you create at home, and where you go.

Then there was ***Stella***, whom I met at one of our local Zero-Waste Workshops, and she was positively beaming. After she set up her house to be as close to zero-waste as she could, Stella was prepared to tackle other areas of her life. She started commuting by bicycle, bus, and/or train instead of jumping into her car, continuing on with her carbon waste reduction, and she didn't stop there. Stella bulk-bought, avoided packaging where possible, and even carried her own bags and jars. So effectively, her pantry was free of plastic, her shopping bags were reusable, and her kitchen waste was composted, turning possible landfall into nutrients to feed her thriving garden.

Stella's closet also appeared very different. She utilized the capsule wardrobe method in which she collected versatile, high-quality clothing that could be mixed and matched, thus avoiding the need to buy constantly. This was one way not only to cut on waste and remove clutter but also to add simplicity to her life, saving time and money.

Every step Stella took was a personal commitment to a zero-waste life, and her life, as it were, was the embodiment of a sustainable testimony of its values. It would be watching her conscious personal efforts start to ripple across the landscape, igniting that spark. Her enthusiasm was catching, and she made other people think about their environmental footprint.

Now, think for a minute what it feels like to know that each choice you make carries profound environmental impacts. Think, instead, you picked the local café serving fair trade, organic coffee two blocks away from the place that is not organic and not fair trade. How about the way you clean your house?

But going zero-waste at home can start one in the direction of the expansion of choices around the lifestyle that is enriching to the planet and one's life. In reality, living simply and more intentionally creates unforeseen freedom and clarity, which enables a person to focus on meaningful connections, personal growth, and active community engagement.

Personally, these practices have brought about a tremendous change in my life. Living in a zero-waste home teaches one that every choice they make is a vote for what kind of world they would like to live in. Just like Stella, I changed my travel habits. Started using public transport and sharing cars. Getting connected with local environmentalist groups turned out to be full of satisfaction and also extended my contacts. Through this experience, it became clear that the zero-waste lifestyle, contrary to all expectations, is more about community than it is about personal acts. Sharing experiences, tips, and challenges with fellow enthusiasts serves to keep my motivation up, yet it multiplies the impact of our efforts.

Imagine a future where sustainability is the theme of life, a world in which every decision we make is made considering the welfare of the planet. Transitioning to zero-waste beyond our homes is so much more than just not generating waste; it's a way of contributing to a sustainable, just world. Are you ready for this next phase? Remember, the changes you will make will benefit you in the long run. Let's take our focus outside the home and integrate zero-waste everywhere. Embrace the challenge, the fulfillment of the journey, and the pretty lifestyle that this zero-waste existence brings. Let us all journey toward that future together, full of sustainability and community spirit.

Community and Sharing

As zero-waste becomes part of our routine, community camaraderie is the new empowerment. Now, it is not only for the reduction of waste but also a way to have a tighter bond with one another, enabling our capabilities to make our zero-waste practices sustainable and scalable. Having become conscious consumers and gone zero-waste myself, like Stella, so many of us cannot help but connect with others who are walking a similar path. It can be as simple as joining a local sustainability group, doing a challenge with friends, or even organizing an event to show how other people and communities can help take care of the environment.

Community solidarity is a powerful one, multiplying individual efforts into massive group changes; it radiates out across neighborhoods, cities, and finally, the world, just like ripples in the waters. For example, after her life change, Stella longed to be with like-minded people. She started a local group of concerned citizens that met once a month to share ideas on how to minimize trash in their lives and immediate environment. That group shared more than just tips and where to get this or that alternative. This group went on to organize community projects, such as a neighborhood compost project and a zero-waste fair, to spread the word and get the community involved.

Engaging in such community-based activities also proves rewarding. It creates a sense of belonging and community-mobilized self-esteem that might play an essential role in retaining one in such a lifestyle in the long run. She knew, through the guidance of her community-based organization, that every small activity that she could engage in meant one step closer to a global impact. They were not just reducing waste; they were creating an atmosphere of waste awareness that would motivate and impact the world. Take another success story: I came across this one guy, Tom, a vibrant retiree who had taken his woodworking passion and turned it into a community asset. He started a 'tool library' where people could loan out tools they might only use once or twice rather than owning their own. That was less waste from packaging and tools that sat idle. This also built much stronger community ties.

Neighbors started sharing much more: they shared knowledge and skills, even supporting each other in the improvement of their houses. The library became a more dynamic hub to pull the community together and create a culture of sharing and sustainability. These stories underline the need to build community. A community shares resources but, more importantly, passes along encouragement and inspiration. This could be the key to turning the struggle to live zero-waste from a solo quest into a community win.

Think of it this way: expand that community beyond local boundaries. Today, our community goes beyond time and space with modern technology. By utilizing web platforms, one could get connected to different zero-waste advocates across the globe, hence, with a treasure trove of knowledge and inspiration. With virtual forums, webinars, and online workshops, it is more facilitated to be enriched in the subject and to come across the innovations being practiced in different places of the world. But more importantly, we should share the journey and tell our stories. Each story shared in a blog, a community event, or on social media can set something alight in someone. When I started sharing my personal zero-waste life journey on the internet, I was amazed at the number of people who resonated with me, and many wrote to say they were feeling called to action in the same manner. That just confirmed how powerful our stories are, no matter how small they seem.

Still, it is a process that is time-consuming and requires devotion when creating such a community network. A number of steps to begin with are:

- ***Connect Locally***: Keep an eye out for or establish local groups of interest with a sustainability focus. Local libraries, community centers, and neighborhood cafes are often sites hosting or providing information about such events.
- ***Engage Online***: Join forums, follow blogs, and social media accounts on any of the platforms where zero-waste living is discussed. Not only do they provide informative information,

but they also serve as a point of motivation and a point of solidarity.

- ***Organize Events***: Be it a workshop, a swap meet, or a community clean-up, any events one hosts at the local level can create awareness among a large section of the population and, at the same time, motivate others to undertake zero-waste activities.
- ***Share Your Story***: Discuss your experiences. Try all the available platforms you have at your disposal and share with others what you have learned, the challenges you had to push through, and the victories you have achieved.

As we build these relationships, we build further into the depth and fullness of our lives. In my own experience, I found the more active the involvement on my part, the richer the experience. It's not only drawing from the collective wisdom and strength of the community but also contributing to an ever-growing force that can make a real difference to the environment. Indeed, possibilities are limitless. We all inspire and collaborate with other members of our community by sharing our stories to contribute to a planet that will become more sustainable. Indeed, it is not only about waste reduction; this speaks more of leaving an earth well taken care of and one that future generations will enjoy.

So let us, as we put zero-waste principles into play through each arena of our lives, raise the bar higher in regard to deepening our support in order to increase our impact. Let us make sure that our efforts to be sustainable people are not for personal success but for the world revolution. Are you ready to make this leap and keep on walking along this path? Count me in!

Continuing Your Zero-Waste Journey

What emerges from the zero-waste home is the landscape of opportunities and challenges. Now, as we build our networks and learn from each other, the natural next step is to just keep pushing forward, diving in deep to understand and perfect our practices. The journey toward a sustainable lifestyle has to be continuous and marked not only by achievements but also by *growth and learning.* That necessarily entails commitment and will to constantly be in the relentless pursuit of new knowledge and experience. Being ready for change must be applied not only to the way we manage our waste but to the way we think about our lives in every area. Every decision we make, from the food we choose to eat to our travel plans, offers a chance to cause a change for good. In my own journey, the first steps were dedicated to waste reduction literally inside my home: switching to reusables, learning to compost, and finding creative ways to reuse items. But with every layer I peeled away, what seemed to become apparent to me was that sustaining this lifestyle entailed not only maintaining these practices but also expanding my knowledge and skills.

Continuing the Journey with Lifelong Learning

I will keep journeying with lifelong learning.

Education and continued learning are the bases of long-term change. As we move forward, we have to nurture our curiosity and commitment to a zero-waste lifestyle. This could be done by keeping up with the latest research in sustainability through workshops and conferences or even taking courses in areas related to zero-waste, such as organic farming, sustainable fashion, or renewable energy alternatives.

Learning is a never-ending process, and that is exactly what has transformed my life. All my learning experiences, be it from reading, documentaries, or hands-on workshops, have expanded my mind over the possibilities and issues in the zero-waste movement. I recently subscribed to an online permaculture course, which takes me through the amazing change that is beginning to shape our agricultural and social design, mimicking the patterns in natural ecosystems. It was an experience that kept on teaching me about food-growing methods and brought into light the journey to create homes and communities that are more in tune with nature. And to see how those little pieces do add up—really add up—to a massive, great, green-living story just really hit home and created an even greater drive to be more mindful in living and, therefore, to push even harder for the practice of zero-waste wherever I found the possibility for it.

Sustainability means a lifelong, endless journey that unfolds with each step and is punctuated by new revelations and concerted effort on the part of the entire community. Navigating the zero-waste lifestyle converts every new insight or experiment into a way of leveling up the quality of our lives and becoming guiding beacons for those interested in starting or expanding their very own journey into sustainability.

Continuing with Passion and Purpose

Think of it as a growing roadmap of potential: Open this book and find a path to discovery and enlightenment. Now, in the depth of this journey toward zero waste, your ability to make a difference grows gradually from your individual practice to collective and on to affect more than we could ever have imagined. Making knowledge and successes from your journey accessible and using your voice to influence systems are parts of it, but so is being a part of creating the results yourself.

For example, having come to the awareness that homemade beeswax candles have had the effect of proving a relatively strong deterrent to dependence upon mainstream traditional solutions to lighting, I conducted several community-based workshops on how to create homemade and eco-friendly candles. In addition to learning how to illuminate living spaces in an increasingly sustainable manner, the workshops themselves opened up dialogue with respect to energy consumption and the degree to which such consumption ultimately has a negative impact on the environment with regard to traditional forms of lighting.

And much the same, driven by the element of sustainability and multiplicity that is harbored within those seed paper greeting cards and by nurturing the green practices, I shared this initiative with local schools by setting up art projects centered around the same creation of seed paper art. Some of them fostered the topic of artistic expression, some pointed out the value of biodiversity, and some showed how plants take part in climate change resolution.

More than that, with the added benefit of the herbal potpourri sachets to improve indoor air quality and thereby decrease the reliance on synthetic air fresheners, I was increasingly motivated to bring sachets into local businesses and public places. Indeed, such sachets filled space with natural scents and even prompted others to hold discussions regarding the need for adopting natural alternatives in everyday life. In other words, every make toward zero-waste is inspirational in its own way; it illuminates the way towards big changes. Through meaningful action and advocacy, we will spread the ripples of our work into communities and beyond, creating a future where sustainability is not something to aspire to but a way of life.

The Next Steps on Your Journey

As you work along the path towards zero-waste, seek new opportunities that continue your learning and sharing with others. Consider these enriching steps:

Delve into Specific Subjects: Be it on sustainable agriculture, renewable energy solutions, or ethical fashion, get yourself engrossed in topics that you find interesting. This may provide insight and open possible doors to new careers.

If one were to become interested in sustainable agriculture, one would, therefore, deeply delve into the principles of permaculture through workshops and online courses; the understanding of regenerative agricultural practices would be way stronger. This type of specialized knowledge will empower you to make informed choices about food production and land stewardship.

❖ ***Explore New Practices:***

Constantly try new zero-waste practices. You could attempt to make your own cosmetics or maintain a garden. The lessons learned from each new approach are reality-centered and could bring new, unexpected, and very fitting solutions.

For example, you can make your own natural skincare products with ingredients like coconut oil and shea butter, which will save on packaging waste and most likely educate you more directly about customized solutions that resonate with your values and preferences.

❖ ***Engage with Experts:***

Reach out to people who have experience and expertise in the field of sustainability that you are interested in. Seek their mentorship for customized insights and a way forward in the labyrinth of the adopted zero-waste lifestyle.

For example, you could look up to local environmentalists who have specialized in renewable energy solutions. With this in mind, their knowledge will guide you on how to best personalize advice on the use of sustainable technologies such as solar panels or wind turbines in your life.

- ***Share your Knowledge:***

Share this experience and the knowledge you have acquired with others, for example, in workshops, and on social media. Teaching not only serves to enforce understanding of the problem but also, according to experience, is a perfect method of motivating and empowering others to take steps on their own path toward sustainability.

For example, you could also make a blog about it to document his/her zero-waste journey and post useful tips on how to reduce environmental impacts for everybody else. This is one way of sharing knowledge to inspire and empower others toward sustainable change in their lives.

- ***Reflect and Evolve:***

Take stock of zero-waste practices periodically. What works well, and where could things be done better? Sustainability is not static, so this perpetual stage of evolution and change is a basis for progress.

For example, you would estimate the amount of waste your household produces and probably find out even better ways to reduce your ecological footprint, such as reducing food wastage by composting or living a minimalistic life. These constant evaluations and modifications in your habits will, with time, lead to sustainable and mindful living.

Sharing Your Journey to Inspire Others

After all, your journey can be an inspiration to others, not just from sharing successes and challenges but from *being transparent with life experiences*. This kind of openness doesn't just motivate but also ignites joy and gives strength to those who might have given up after failure at the start of the journey to zero-waste. Your will to share it may reignite their zealousness and foster their resolution of starting afresh. They will have the courage to keep trying until they get it right and attain success. You may also consider making a YouTube channel or vlog so that people are aware and will come together for your community activities. All these present learning opportunities that make you think critically about the best way to communicate and execute sustainable practices across various dimensions. Let us proceed along this path of exploration, learning, and inspiration. With every single step you take, you do not just satisfy the inner you, but you contribute to a larger change that is happening globally. You are their beacon of hope, and they ardently wait for you to guide them to lift themselves and move toward sustainable living.

CONCLUSION

It's really cool for us to be reaching the end stage of that zero-waste journey together, and we take a look back at how far we've really come. Inspiration has been immense, from those very first days of just making small changes in our daily routines to quite how dramatically we've managed to change our living space and perspective. Through our vigilance and resourcefulness, we have not only designed our living spaces but have had a hand in keeping our planet healthy.

But the journey has just begun. There are endless possibilities. Every choice that was made is part of a much bigger movement to make the environment safe. By embracing the values and principles of zero-waste, we have hence positioned ourselves as proactive citizens in the protection of Earth for the generations to follow.

So, what does this exciting path hold for us? Countless opportunities. Be it in the workplace, adopting zero-waste practices, involvement in local environmental projects, or advocating for less damaging alternatives in communities, there is always a chance to do a little bit more to get that message across and stir change.

Remember that challenges are always present, yet they are indeed opportunities for development and innovation. It is your relentless determination that will set the difference in countless ways, and every bit of effort—small or large—will be for a greater future on our planet. As we give thanks for finally starting on this journey, let's take this moment to recommit to exploring, innovating, and working hard to find a better, less wasteful way of living. Here's to embarking on many more adventures in zero-waste living—filled with creativity, camaraderie, and compassion for our environment. Let's be strong in our resolve to have the world a place we are proud to call home. You are thereby paving the way for change by committing to the laborious manual and projects that even tyros may undertake. With every new project you take up, you mature and develop; you gain priceless knowledge and skills in the process. And at the same time, be a part of a cleaner planet, so let's practice and learn more.

This is how this journey has made an impact on me.

I start my morning by planning my day, looking that every work I do keeps in mind my zero-waste. I began by pulling my reusable coffee cup, water bottle, and a set of cloth napkins to load into my bag for the day. As I moved out of the door, I ensured I had taken some shopping bags just in case, when coming back home, there was a need for a quick market stop. I use digital tools actively in taking notes of meetings, which eliminates the need to use papers for such work and ensures that my notes are in an appropriately arranged order of retrieval.

During lunch, I carry food in my own containers, reusable, of course, and that usually gets my coworkers talking about sustainable practices. I use this as an opportunity for myself to spend part of my afternoon finding new ways to achieve zero-waste, like how to make my own natural cleaning products, which I will do this coming weekend. Before leaving, I make sure to print important documents on both sides of the paper in order to save more paper.

Back home, I sort the mail, recycle what is possible, and put the important letters in my mail folder to avoid clutter. I make a zero-waste dinner with ingredients bought in bulk and stored in my glass containers. And now, I can just relax, thinking about all the great things I accomplished today and the ones that gave me problems for tomorrow. There is time to think about how to better and innovate my zero-waste journey. Not only does this add enrichment to my daily activities, but it also benefits the environment, making it one step closer to sustainability.

www.ingramcontent.com/pod-product-compliance
Lightning Source LLC
LaVergne TN
LVHW052341100826
845147LV00021B/1143